Supermarine Spitfire 80

ON THE OCCASION OF THE 80TH ANNIVERSARY OF THE FIRST FLIGH[T]
PROTOTYPE SPITFIRE WE PRESENT A SPECIAL 'FLYPAST' TO CELEBRAT[E]
GREATEST FIGHTER. THIS PUBLICATION IS DEDICATED TO ALL THOS[E]
BUILT, MAINTAINED AND FLEW SPITFIRES; FROM 1936 ALL THE WAY INTO THE 21ST CENTUR[Y]
THE LEGEND LIVES ON.

Image: COL POPE

Supermarine Spitfire 80

CONTENTS

Below right
Across the world restored Spitfires continue to turn heads whenever they take to the air. The Aero Legends Mk.IX TD314 (G-CGYJ) 'St George' in the colours of 234 Squadron getting ready for a sortie from Duxford. COL POPE

Edited by: Ken Ellis
Group Editor: Nigel Price

Art Editor: Mike Carr
Chief Designer: Steve Donovan

Production Editor: Sue Blunt
Deputy Production Editor: Carol Randall
Production Manager: Janet Watkins

Advertisement Manager: Alison Sanders
Advertising Production: Debi McGowan
Group Advertisement Manager: Brodie Baxter

Marketing Executive: Shaun Binnington
Marketing Manager: Martin Steele

Commercial Director: Ann Saundry
Managing Director and Publisher: Adrian Cox
Executive Chairman: Richard Cox

Contacts
Key Publishing Ltd, PO Box 100, Stamford, Lincs, PE9 1XQ.
Tel 01780 755131
Email flypast@keypublishing.com
www.keypublishing.com

Distribution: Seymour Distribution Ltd, 2 Poultry Avenue, London EC1A 9PP. Tel 020 74294000

Printed by: Warners (Midland) plc, The Maltings, Bourne, Lincs, PE10 9PH

Published by: Key Publishing Ltd - see above
Printed in England

WENT THE WELL?

Below
The Supermarine Type 300 ready for Mutt Summers, at Eastleigh, March 1936.
ALL KEY COLLECTION UNLESS NOTED

Miles Falcon Six G-ADTD touched down at Eastleigh on March 5, 1936 on a flight from Martlesham Heath. It was piloted by Jeffrey Quill and with him was his boss, Joseph 'Mutt' Summers, who had had an appointment with a sleek, powerful aircraft that was waiting outside the Supermarine factory – the Type 300, K5054.

Vickers had acquired Supermarine in November 1928, but the Southampton-based company continued to keep its name. As chief test pilot for Vickers, Summers held responsibility for the products of the parent organisation at Brooklands and at Eastleigh, although both sites had 'resident' test pilots: George Pickering looked after production testing for the flying-boats and amphibians. Jeffrey Quill had not long been appointed by Summers as his No.2, across both airfields, although the new fighter was destined to dominate his flying career.

His team faced an increasingly busy time in 1936. Already on Summers' mind was an important project at Brooklands; in 103 day's time he would test fly B92/32 K4049, the nascent Wellington bomber.

The rest of the group had probably arrived from the Supermarine factory at Woolston, on the Solent, in the car used as the backdrop for the quintet. This was a Riley Nine, owned by Reginald Joseph Mitchell, the man who had designed the new prototype. Inevitably nicknamed 'Agony', H J Payn was technical assistant to Mitchell and also a pilot. Stuart Scott-Hall had become a fixture at the drawing office and on the factory floor; he was the Air Ministry's resident technical officer, keeping an eye on the progress of the new fighter project.

Hand-built, the Type 300 was unpainted and without covers to its main undercarriage legs – the gear would stay locked down for the maiden flight. A small crowd of onlookers had assembled; it was an important day for Supermarine and was to turn out to be an incredible day for aviation history. Summers took K5054 into the air and, typical of his inaugural flights, was back in 15 minutes. Clearly well pleased, he is reported as telling the ground crew: "Don't touch anything" – he was that happy with its performance.

SHORT CIRCUIT

Joseph Summers was 32 when he flew the Type 300. He joined the RAF in 1924 and went on to fly with 29 Squadron from Duxford on Sopwith Snipes and later Gloster Grebes. His skills were so good that he was soon posted to the Aeroplane & Armament Experimental Establishment at Martlesham Heath.

With the death of Vickers chief test pilot 'Tiny' Scholefield in May 1929, Summers asked for release to take over at Brooklands, and this was granted. Over the next 22 years

DAY

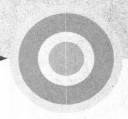

FIVE MEN ALL WITH GOOD REASON TO SMILE – THE PROTOTYPE SPITFIRE HAD JUST FLOWN. **KEN ELLIS** SETS THE SCENE

Left
Informal gathering at Eastleigh after the first flight of the Spitfire prototype, March 5, 1936. Left to right: 'Mutt' Summers, H J 'Agony' Payn, R J Mitchell, Stuart Scott-Hall and Jeffrey Quill. KEC

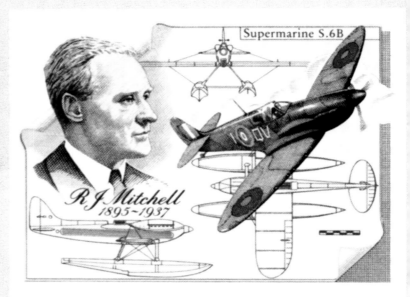

> "AFTER THE FIRST FLIGHT OF THE SPITFIRE MITCHELL WAS BUOYED UP BY THE PLAUDITS OF BOTH COMPANY TEST PILOTS AND FROM THE 'CUSTOMERS' AT MARTLESHAM HEATH. ALL THE WHILE, HIS HEALTH WAS DETERIORATING, BUT THERE WAS MUCH TO DO..."

Summers took his tally of prototypes to 29, his portfolio running from biplanes, flying-boats, the Spitfire and Wellington to the turboprop Viscount airliner and the Valiant V-bomber.

Maiden flights were almost exclusively short, a classic Summers quick 'circuit'. Summers believed that inaugural sorties should be just so, proving that the type could aviate; the detailed, exacting test schedule was for the following days and months. He was a great at lifting everyone's morale with the success of a 'first'; leaving any damning analysis to another day.

With responsibilities across both Supermarine and Vickers products, Summers conducted first flights and initial trials on the final flying-boats from the Woolston stable. The last of the line was the Southampton V which had its debut in July 1934 and was renamed Stranraer in August 1935.

It was the Seagull V pusher amphibian for the Royal Australian Air Force, which Summers took on its maiden flight in June 1933, that had been the most important Supermarine programme until the Spitfire changed everything. Summers made enquiries with Mitchell about the strength of the Seagull V's airframe and then surprised everyone – including its designer – by *looping* the prototype at the Hendon airshow, *four* days after

the maiden flight! The RAF and Fleet Air Arm (FAA) adopted the type from April 1935 and named it Walrus.

From the first flight of the Wellington, on June 15, 1936, the demands of two expanding programmes meant that Summers turned almost exclusively to all things Brooklands, leaving Quill to take on the considerable challenge of developing what was to become the Spitfire 'family'. Barnes Wallis was the design supremo at Brooklands and his fertile mind was focused on special weapons, including the famous 'Bouncing Bombs' for the Dams raid of May 1943. In the run-up to this, Summers was heavily involved in development of the Upkeep 'mine' and the later Highball anti-shipping weapon, at first in Wellingtons and later in Avro Lancasters.

With the age of radio allowing for increased communication between test pilot and the anxious design staff, Summers devised a code to convey his thoughts and to throw anyone 'eavesdropping' off the scent. He often reported "swithering" which sounded dire, but actually meant that all was well.

Soon after captaining the maiden flight of the prototype four-jet Valiant V-bomber on May 18, 1951 – for a near traditional 18 minutes – Summers handed over to his deputy,

Jock Bryce. At that point he had over 5,000 hours in an astonishing 366 types. Mutt Summers CBE died following a stomach operation on March 16, 1954 – six days after his 50th birthday.

UTMOST SECURITY

H J Payn was commissioned into the Royal Engineers by 1915, transferring to the Royal Flying Corps in 1916. By February 1917 he was serving on the Western Front with 29 Squadron, flying Airco DH.2s alongside James McCudden. On February 23, 1916 Payn was on the receiving end of the guns of an Albatros piloted by Werner Voss – Payn escaped with damage to his DH.2. Payn left the RAF in 1923 as a squadron leader and joined the staff of Vickers.

With an excellent background in engineering, Payn was appointed as technical assistant to Vickers chief designer Rex Pierson at Brooklands. He was also involved in flight testing whenever his services were required.

When Vickers bought Supermarine, Payn was seconded to Woolston and by 1930 was an executive with the company, acting as R J Mitchell's technical assistant. When Mitchell died in June 1937, Rex Pierson was given overall charge of the design offices at both Brooklands and Woolston. Payn was appointed as

manager of the design department of Supermarine.

In his exceptional *Spitfire - A Test Pilot's Story*, Quill describes a disturbing facet of Britain's increasing worry about security, particularly on a vital programme such as the Spitfire. "Payn came under investigation by the security services as a result of a divorce and re-marriage to a lady of foreign origin. The immediate and direct result was that the Air Ministry withdrew their approval for Payn to hold his position of high responsibility in an area where security was obviously of the utmost importance." Payn was dismissed and his considerable skills were denied to the war effort.

TRANSFORMING GENIUS

The strains of getting an advanced prototype ready for its maiden flight certainly contributed towards Mitchell's grey complexion on March 5, 1936, but there was another reason for the pallor. Three years before, the 41-year-old had been diagnosed with a cancer that medical knowledge was then ill-equipped to combat. He took this with a degree of stoicism, all the while working his customary long hours.

Close friends and colleagues were allowed to call him 'RJ' and by the time the Type 300 flew, Mitchell's skills had transformed the prospects of Supermarine. Born in 1885 at Talke, a village near Stoke-on-Trent, he left school at 16 and was apprenticed to Kerr, Stuart and Company. Learning at the workbench and in the drawing office, he was laying the foundations of his double mastery of the theory and practice of engineering.

Aviation fascinated Mitchell; he was determined to join this new industry. In 1916, his opportunity came; he was taken on as a draughtsman at Supermarine. Three years later chief designer F J Hargreaves, resigned. Supermarine appointed RJ in his place – this was a bold move as he was only 24, but it was obvious to all around him how talented and conscientious he was. In 1920, the company's faith in him was cemented when he was promoted to chief engineer, and in 1927 he was made a director.

It would take a book to chronicle each and every one of Mitchell's creations. *Winning Streak* on page 16 deals with the stuff of legend that was the Schneider Trophy story. This entire venture was much more than 'flag-waving'; it gave Mitchell the leap of technology that was to make the Spitfire possible.

The military Seagull biplane amphibian series began in 1922 helping to break the small company out of the hand-to-mouth existence of previous years. Up until 1924, Supermarine had concentrated on single-engined marine aircraft, but in that year it created its first twin-engined type, the commercial Swan amphibian. This paved the way for the Southampton flying-boat

'family' from 1925, to be followed by the Scapa and the Stranraer. The last amphibian that Mitchell worked on was intended to succeed the Walrus; the Sea Otter had its maiden flight in 1938 but it was not until 1943 that it entered limited production.

Supermarine and Mitchell had little experience of monoplanes but through the Schneider competitions each had gained command of advanced aerodynamics and construction techniques. This meant that Specification F7/30 for a single-seat day fighter, ideally powered by a Rolls-Royce Goshawk with evaporative cooling, was well within the grasp of the company.

The gull-winged, faired undercarriage, open cockpit, Type 224 first flew in February 1934 and proved disappointing from the very

Works at Southampton on September 26, 1940.

Reginald Joseph Mitchell CBE died on June 11, 1937. Up to the last he had been poring over calculations and layouts to put cannons into the wing of the Spitfire.

His passing was a devastating blow to the creative team at Supermarine. RJ had always praised those around him and his quiet, industrious manner engendered great loyalty. His deputy, Joseph 'Joe' Smith stepped into the breech and from his ingenious mind and thorough adherence to the Mitchell design philosophy, all of the Spitfire variants sprang.

Greatest testament to RJ is the Spitfire, but it cannot be emphasized too much that the regime in the engineering and design offices was such that after the mourning, they

the post of assistant to Summers.

At Brooklands there were Vildebeests and Vincents to test, and Wellesleys would start to come off the production line in the spring of 1937. On February 5, 1936 Quill was at Woodley where he carried out an acceptance flight on Falcon Six G-ADTD which was the new 'taxi', particularly for flying down to Eastleigh where the Spitfire was being readied. Twenty-one days after Summers carried out the maiden flight of K5054, Quill piloted the gleaming prototype – this was the start of a unique association, he went on to fly every Spitfire and Seafire variant.

Promoted as chief test pilot for Supermarine in May 1938, on the 14th Quill conducted the maiden flight of K9787, the second Spitfire. Getting production flowing was a

Right
Jeffrey Quill piloting K8054 during night flying trials, 1936.

start. None of the bidders for F7/30 were successful and in the end the requirement was re-written as F14/35 and won by the Gloster Gladiator, destined to be the RAF's last biplane fighter.

LASTING LEGACY
Perhaps the F7/30 gave RJ the determination to plough his own furrow. The Type 300 was the accumulation of all that he and his design, structures, aerodynamics and engineering teams had learned.

After the first flight of the Spitfire Mitchell was buoyed up by the plaudits of both company test pilots and from the 'customers' at Martlesham Heath. All the while, his health was deteriorating, but there was much to do...

In September 1936 he created the Supermarine response to Specification B12/36 for a long-range strategic bomber. It featured elliptical wings and, as might be expected, it was a good-looking aeroplane. The two prototypes were destroyed in the devastating air raid on the Itchen

got straight down to work. Mitchell's management style was inspirational, not dictatorial. He and the rest of his team had come up with a fighter that would help defeat dictatorship and inspire generations into the 21st century.

EVERY VARIANT
While Mutt Summers took the accolade of the first flight of the Type 300, there are two names that will be forever linked with the development and mass manufacture of the Spitfire – Jeffery Quill and Alex Henshaw (see page 52) respectively. Jeffrey took on the bulk of the trials flying and he created and managed the large production test organisation required to meet the output.

On November 1, 1935, Flt Lt Quill flew an Armstrong Whitworth Siskin to Brooklands to have a word with Summers about a job with Vickers. He had joined the RAF in 1931 and in 1934 became the commanding officer of the RAF Meteorological Flight at Duxford. After another, more formal, meeting at Brooklands, Quill accepted

traumatic experience – see page 52 – and it was the Castle Bromwich Aircraft Factory that was to transform the creation of Spitfires.

After the bombing of the Woolston factory in September 1940 a dispersed production system was introduced. At the same time, Worthy Down was taken over as the main centre for development and production testing. Quill arranged for 'sample' aircraft from other factories to be brought to Worthy Down to check on quality.

Thousands of hours of testing delivered many dramatic moments, but only one sortie ended in a write-off. Flying the interim Mk.21 prototype DP851 on May 13, 1943, the starboard undercarriage failed on landing at Boscombe Down; the aircraft whipped around, removing the port leg in the process. Travelling on its belly backwards, the Mk.21 was beyond repair when it came to stop; Quill was unhurt.

'HANDS ON'
Trained as a fighter pilot, Quill first served with 17 Squadron, flying

Bristol Bulldog IIs, at Upavon in September 1932. He put great pressure on the RAF to be allowed to join an operational Spitfire squadron so he could appreciate how he could help make the fighter exactly what its pilots were looking for. The logic of his request was eventually recognised, and on August 5, 1940 – at the height of the Battle of Britain – Flt Lt Quill was attached to 65 Squadron at Hornchurch.

He made it clear he was not just an observer. On the 16th he shot down a Messerschmitt Bf 109E and two days later shared in the downing of a Heinkel He 111. Quill returned to Eastleigh on August 24.

This 'hands-on' attitude extended to the FAA in early 1944. Other than a couple of landings on HMS *Indomitable*, Quill had little experience of aircraft carriers, yet he was testing a fighter designed to do just that. He was appointed as a supernumerary Lieutenant Commander and by the spring of 1944 was at Easthaven to experience the delights of aerodrome dummy deck landings.

Quill went on to spend an intensive time with the FAA, flying Seafire IIs with 879 and 886 Squadrons, from HMS *Attacker* and *Ravager* and the trials carrier *Pretoria Castle*.

BIPLANE TO TORNADO
Joe Smith's ultimate development of the Spitfire was so much of a transformation that it was renamed: Spiteful for the RAF and Seafang for the FAA. The Spiteful provided the means for Supermarine, and Quill, to make the transition to jets in the form of the Attacker naval fighter.

By marrying the Spiteful wing and undercarriage to a new fuselage, the first operational Royal Navy jet fighter, the Attacker, was born. Jeffrey conducted the debut of TS409 from Boscombe Down on July 27, 1946. Having inaugurated the jet age for Supermarine, the following year Quill handed over the chief test pilot post to his friend and colleague Mike Lithgow.

Jeffrey Quill OBE AFC went on to an impressive career with Vickers and, from 1960, the British Aircraft Corporation, concluding as Director of Marketing at Panavia: during his working life he had evolved from Bulldog biplanes to swing-wing Tornados.

At one stage in the war, the press called him 'Hell-Diver Quill' which the quiet, modest pilot must have hated. After his death on February 20, 1996 at the age of 83, Jeffery Quill was universally referred to as 'Mr Spitfire' with deep respect and affection. ●

IN THEIR ELEMENT

FROM MK.I TO MK.XIX AND SEAFIRES, RENOWNED PHOTOGRAPHER **JOHN DIBBS** HAS CAPTURED THEM ALL – AIR-TO-AIR. THROUGHOUT THIS SPECIAL PUBLICATION, WE PRESENT A PORTFOLIO OF JOHN'S TRIBUTE TO SUPERMARINE'S MASTERPIECE

John Dibbs established the Plane Picture Company in 1993 and since then he has carried more than 1,000 air-to-air sorties. He has had countless images published, produced a range of superbly executed books and every year his 'Flying Legends' calendar is much sought-after. On October 3, 2015, high over Coningsby, Lincolnshire, John caught this incredible formation on the occasion of the Battle of Britain Memorial Flight's end-of-season event. This was Sqn Ldr 'Dunc' Mason's final sortie as officer commanding BBMF. Piloting Spitfire IIa P7350, he led Spitfires and Hurricanes from the Flight and several 'friends' for the occasion.

For more on John's work, an incredible image gallery and even downloads, take a look at www. planepicture.com

FIRST OF THE
BATTLE OF B

After an agonising wait, it was not until May 14, 1938 before a second Spitfire took to the air, Mk.I K9787 in the hands of Jeffrey Quill. Getting the Spitfire into production had proven to be a traumatic experience for the company, which was more used to building small batches of flying-boats and amphibians.

Designer R J Mitchell's prototype differed little from the Mk.I. Power came from a Merlin II with 'ejector' exhausts and not flush stubs; the rudder horn balancing had been altered and gone was the archaic tail skid.

The Spitfire became operational in August 1938 when 19 Squadron at Duxford began exchanging

SPITFIRE I FACTFILE

The seventh Mk.I built, K9793 was issued to the Aeroplane & Armament Experimental Establishment at Martlesham Heath on September 9, 1938 and was used for trials with a de Havilland metal three-bladed propeller. KEY COLLECTION

Engine: Rolls-Royce Merlin II or III of 900hp (738kW)
Statistics: Dimensions: Span 36ft 10in (11.23m) Length 29ft 11in (9.12m) Height 8ft 2¼in (2.5m)
Weights: Empty 4,341lb (1,969kg) Loaded 5,720lb (2,595kg) Performance: Max speed 367mph (591km/h) Service Ceiling 34,500ft (10.51m)
Armament: Mk.Ia eight 0.303in machine guns; Mk.Ib two 20mm cannon, plus four 0.303in machine guns
First flown: May 14, 1938, K9787 flown by Jeffrey Quill at Eastleigh
Number built: 1,427 by Supermarine and Westland
Sub-Variants: Mk.Ia and Mk.Ib armament options. Series of photo-recce conversions, PR.Ia to PR.Ig; the PR.Ic to PR.Ig were re-designated as PR.III, PR.IV, PR.V, PR.VI and PR.VII in 1941 but should not be confused with the Mk.III to Mk.VII. One-offs: High Speed Spitfire; Floatplane.

MANY
TAIN WARRIOR

Gloster Gauntlet biplanes for Mk.Is – K9789 was handed over on the 4th. Despite all of the problems in starting to mass produce Spitfires, Supermarine had managed to complete the first production order, for 310, by the time war broke out. By July 1940 there were enough for 19 operational squadrons, ready for the Luftwaffe's onslaught.

The last Mk.Is rolled off the Westland assembly line at Yeovil in late 1941.

Left

Just 72 hours separates the end of the flying careers of a pair of magnificently recreated Mk.Is. Defending the withdrawal from the Dunkirk beaches on May 25, 1940 Plt Off Peter Casenove was flying Mk.I P9374 (foreground and also below) of 92 Squadron. Casenove made a force landing on the beach at Calais; P9374 has been with the unit since early March and had clocked just 32 flying hours. Three days later, Mk.I N3200 of 19 Squadron also came down on the beach near Calais. In 1980 and 1986 respectively, the two hulks were salvaged and both eventually came to the Duxford workshops of Historic Flying. There they were transformed and P9374 (G-MKIA) flew again in 2011 and N3200 (G-CFGJ) in 2014. JOHN M DIBBS – PLANE PICTURE COMPANY

G.H. Stainforth.

J Boothman

WINNING STREAK

DANIEL FORD SHOWS HOW THE SUPERMARINE RACING FLOATPLANES PROVED THE TECHNOLOGY FOR THE SPITFIRE

Above
The outright winning 1931 entrant S.6B S1595 afloat on the Solent, September 1931. It is signed by its pilot, Flt Lt John Boothman (right) and the world air speed record holder, Flt Lt George Stainforth. ALL AUTHOR'S COLLECTION UNLESS NOTED

Right
R J Mitchell (centre) with pilots of the RAF High Speed Flight at Calshot, September 1931.

They'd not turned up. The RAF High Speed Flight was readying its men and aircraft at Calshot Spit on the Solent in early September 1931, but teams from France and Italy were conspicuous by their absence. Since 1913 various nations had fought for the beautiful trophy conceived by French engineering and armaments magnate Jacques Schneider.

The aim was to encourage aerodynamic and engineering progress by competing seaplanes against the clock, around a closed-circuit course. France hosted the first race in April 1913. Each time, the winning nation would host the next event. A country that won three consecutive events would take the Schneider Trophy in perpetuity and

the contest would be at an end.

As can be seen from the panel, the British had won in 1927 and 1929 and so the 1931 event would clinch it. But there was nobody to fly against. The rules were scrutinised, Schneider, who had died three years previously, had declared that should other entrants fall by the wayside, it was sufficient for the 'last-man-standing' to carry out a 'fly-over' of the course. Provided there were no infringements or accidents, the trophy would be awarded.

This was not without precedent. At Venice in September 1920 the home team was the only one operational. Luigi Bologna flew a Savoia S.12 flying boat biplane around seven laps centred on the San Andrea naval air station to take the honours.

OUTRIGHT VICTORY

The weather took a hand at Calshot and the 'race' for September 12 was postponed. It would be ironic for Britain to be on the verge of outright victory only to have it snatched away by the climate. On the morning of the 13th all was set fair and Flt Lt John Boothman manoeuvred S.6B S1596 out on to the Solent, gunned the throttle of the 2,300hp (1,715kW) Rolls-Royce 'R' V-12 and flew the course centred off the pier at Ryde on the Isle of Wight flawlessly.

Boothman averaged 340.08mph (547.29km/h) and simultaneously took the 100km close-circuit record at 342.87mph.

Frenchman Maurice Prévost had clattered around the Monaco course

at the very first contest in 1913, piloting a 160hp Deperdussin floatplane at 45.75mph. Thanks to the vision of Jacques Schneider, the state-of-the-art performance had increased by very nearly 300mph in just 18 years.

The Schneider Trophy was Britain's for ever and it is on show at the Science Museum in London, alongside S.6B S1595. (At the Solent Sky museum in Southampton, S.6A N248 is displayed.) The

RAF High Speed Flight did not rest on its laurels on September 13, 1931; that afternoon Flt Lt George Stainforth piloted S1596 to 379.05mph taking the world air speed record. Not content with this, 16 days later Stainforth flew S1595 at 407.5mph, upping the record and becoming the first pilot over the 'magic' 400 figure.

SCHNEIDER LEGACY

The legend of the three-in-a-row victory tends to overshadow British perceptions of other Schneider victories. While designer Reginald Joseph Mitchell ('RJ') was delighted

by the performance of the Supermarine 'S' series, he could reflect that he'd seen it all before.

Supermarine entered the 1919 Schneider contest, held at Bournemouth, to show off the new company's capabilities but its Sea Lion was wrecked. Appointed in rapid succession as chief designer and chief engineer, RJ refined the Sea Lion and in August 1922 test pilot Henri Biard took it to victory at 145mph around the Naples course. ➲

BRITAIN AND THE SCHNEIDER TROPHY

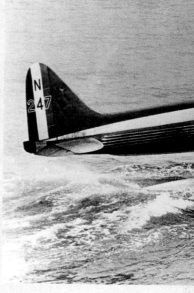

1913 Monaco France and USA
1st   Maurice Prévost, France   Deperdussin   45.75mph (73.62km/h)

1914 Monaco France, Great Britain, Switzerland, USA
1st   Howard Pixton, Great Britain   Sopwith Tabloid   86.78mph (139.65km/h)

1919 Bournemouth France, Italy, Great Britain
No pilot completed the course correctly; Italy was awarded the right to host the next contest.

1920 Venice Italy only
1st   Luigi Bologna, Italy   Savoia S.12   107.22mph (172.56km/h)

1921 Venice France and Italy
1st   Giovanni de Briganti, Italy   Macchi M.7   117.85mph (189.67km/h)

1922 Naples Great Britain and Italy
1st   Henri Biard, Great Britain   Supermarine Sea Lion II G-EBAH   145.72mph (234.51km/h)

1923 Cowes France, Great Britain, USA
1st   Lt David Rittenhouse, USA   Curtiss CR-3   177.37mph (285.45km/h)

1925 Baltimore Great Britain, Italy, USA
1st   Lt James Doolittle, USA   Curtiss R3C-2   232.56mph (374.27km/h)

1926 Hampton Roads Italy and USA
1st   Major Mario de Barnardi, Italy   Macchi M.39   246.49mph (396.69km/h)

1927 Venice Great Britain and Italy
1st   Flt Lt S N Webster, Great Britain   Supermarine S.5 N220   281.55mph (453.28km/h)

1929 Calshot Great Britain and Italy
1st   Fg Off H R D Waghorn, Great Britain   Supermarine S.6 N247   328.62mph (528.87km/h)

1931 Calshot Great Britain only
1st   Flt Lt John Boothman, Great Britain   Supermarine S.6B S1595   340.08mph (547.29km/h)

Also: Flt Lt George Stainforth piloted S1596 to 379.05mph (610.00km/h) taking the world air speed record on the afternoon of the contest, September 13, 1931. On the 29th Stainforth extended this, flying S1595 to 407.5mph.

Just six years later, Supermarine was back with a machine a quantum leap away from the single-seat biplane flying boat. The accomplishments of the 'S' series are well known but what tends to be forgotten is how well the British aircraft industry — airframe, engine, equipment and fuel — combined to pour its talents into the competition. When government backing vaporised for the 1931 contest, the 'private venture' spirit surfaced.

The mid-winged cantilever S.4, designed and built in just *five* months, took off from the Solent on August 24, 1925. Biard disliked its layout, but it was its *concept* that

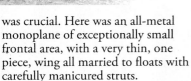

was crucial. Here was an all-metal monoplane of exceptionally small frontal area, with a very thin, one piece, wing all married to floats with carefully manicured struts.

FIGHTER OF THE FUTURE

From the problematic S.4, the Napier Lion-powered low-wing S.5 led the way to the definitive S.6. Mitchell's incredible attention to detail showed everywhere. The floats held fuel and the top surfaces acted as coolant radiators while the oil cooling system ran down the fuselage sides. On the S.6B there was more fuel in the starboard float

to counter the phenomenal torque from the Rolls-Royce 'R' engine. Remove the floats from the S.6, install an undercarriage, and RJ had achieved a fighter of the future.

Boothman's 'fly-over' of the 1931 Schneider course was not a hollow victory. The British aviation industry had received the sort of technological boost normally only associated with the urgency of a war. The experience boosted knowledge in all manner of specialities, including aerodynamics and the problems of 'flutter', wind tunnels, fuel mixtures, 'new' metals and coolants.

Above all, the last three

Schneider Trophy contests vividly demonstrated the strengths and potential of Rolls-Royce and Supermarine. With the 'S' series, the two companies had shown what could be achieved when not fettered by unambitious, or unachievable, Air Ministry specifications.

Rolls-Royce had the basis of a V-12 dynasty for fighters and bombers of the 1940s. Supermarine had made the leap from master of the dying art of flying boats to champion of high speed dynamics. Thanks to its gifted chief engineer, R J Mitchell, the Southampton company was ready to produce a super-fighter. ●

> "...THE LAST THREE SCHNEIDER TROPHY CONTESTS VIVIDLY DEMONSTRATED THE STRENGTHS AND POTENTIAL OF ROLLS-ROYCE AND SUPERMARINE. WITH THE 'S' SERIES, THE TWO COMPANIES HAD SHOWN WHAT COULD BE ACHIEVED WHEN NOT FETTERED BY UNAMBITIOUS, OR UNACHIEVABLE, AIR MINISTRY SPECIFICATIONS."

HONING THE BREED
FROM DEFENC

The Spitfire proved to be a remarkably adaptable airframe. Engine and armament improvements and, most importantly, combat experience contributed to a constantly evolving development programme. Just as the Battle of Britain broke out, Mk.IIs started being issued to units.

With greater power from a Merlin XII, the Mk.II was the domain of the massive Castle Bromwich factory. Based at

SPITFIRE II FACTFILE

Engine:	Rolls-Royce Merlin XII of 1,140hp (850kW)
Statistics:	Dimensions: Span 36ft 10in (11.23m) Length 29ft 11in (9.12m) Height 8ft 2¼in (2.5m) Weights: Empty 4,783lb (2,170kg) Loaded 6,725lb (1,913kg) Performance: Max speed 354mph (570km/h) Service ceiling 37,600ft (11.46m)
Armament:	Mk.IIa eight 0.303in machine guns; Mk.IIb two 20mm cannon, plus four 0.303in machine guns
First flown:	February 1939 using converted Mk.I K9791. First production Mk.II, P7280, issued for trials June 1940
Number built:	920 by Castle Bromwich Aircraft Factory
Sub-Variants:	Mk.IIa and Mk.IIb armament options; Mk.IIc (later ASR.II) air-sea rescue conversions

Built at Castle Bromwich in March 1941, Mk.II P8077 entered service with its fourth unit, 19 Squadron, at Fowlmere on August 21. It is illustrated during rare use of auxiliary underwing 'slipper' tanks. KEY COLLECTION

TO OFFENCE

Warmwell, 152 Squadron was the first with the new variant. The bulk of production was devoted to the eight-gun Mk.IIa, but the Mk.IIb offered the punch of a pair of 20mm cannon and four 0.303in machine guns.

By the end of 1940 Mk.IIs were being used to take the fight back over the Channel, on massed fighter sweeps. The last Mk.IIs were delivered in the summer of 1941, by which time the Mk.V had got into its stride.

Above
The aircraft of the Battle of Britain Memorial Flight (BBMF) change their markings every so often to honour pilots and units of different eras and theatres. Known on the Flight as the 'Baby Spitfire' or 'P7', this machine graces our cover. Mk.IIa P7350 was built at Castle Bromwich, entering service with 266 Squadron at Wittering in September 1940. The following month P7350 was transferred to 603 (City of Edinburgh) Squadron and on October 25, 1940 it was being flown by Polish Plt Off Ludwig Martel. 'Bounced' by Messerschmitt Bf 109s, P7350 was one of four 603 machines brought down; Plt Off Martel effecting a skilful wheels-up forced-landing. Repaired, P7350 re-entered service and was saved in 1948 by the sharp eyes of an employee of scrap merchant John Dale Ltd. It was presented back to the RAF, joining BBMF in late 1968. From 1999, P7350 wore the 603 Squadron codes 'XT-D', but in the spring of 2006 photographer John Dibbs arranged for it to briefly carry the 'XT-W', the markings it wore when Plt Off Martel was shot down. JOHN M DIBBS – PLANE PICTURE COMPANY

MILESTONES

CHARTING THE DEVELOPMENT AND EVOLUTION OF BRITAIN'S GREATEST FIGHTER

Hawker Hart K3036 served as the flying test-bed for the PV.12/Merlin. ROLLS-ROYCE

Countless words have been written on the exploits of Spitfire pilots, the endeavours of their groundcrew and the plans and strategies of the 'top brass', including previous Battle of Britain and Spitfire 'special' publications from *FlyPast*. Less appreciated is the step-by-step development of an incredible family of fighters; how the Spitfire adapted to deal with different adversaries and new tactics and how its designers reacted to the experience gleaned in combat and from emerging technologies.

Little is known about the clamour to purchase, and in some cases to licence build, Spitfires by a large number of European countries as part of rearmament to meet the threat of Hitler's Germany. Even in its earliest days, the Spitfire was seen as a vital counter to the Messerschmitt Bf 109. Had things been different and war not broken out, it seems that Supermarine faced a very healthy export market.

When peace returned, the type was still much in demand and large orders books, for new and reconditioned examples were placed. Details of both of these market places can be found in this guide, as can a reminder of the many countries that flew Spitfires and fought within the RAF during the war. Far from 'standing alone', Britain was bolstered by men and women from many nations.

While some combat highlights are given in this chronological examination of the Spitfire's evolution, we present here the incredible story of how a fighter designed in the mid-1930s could continue in production into the late 1940s and fly operationally for another decade.

1933
Oct 25: Rolls-Royce started ground-runs of its private-venture V12 engine, designated PV.12.

1934
Nov 16: Air Ministry specification F5/34 was issued seeking a single-seat interceptor. Among the requirements were a spritely rate of climb, six or eight guns, retractable undercarriage and an enclosed cockpit. Several companies responded, but beyond a handful of prototypes, no production order was placed. After a design conference Hawker and Supermarine received revised specifications for what were initially private-venture designs: F36/34 for what became the Hurricane and F37/34 for the Spitfire.

Dec 1: A single Supermarine Type 300 prototype was ordered by the Air Ministry.

1935
Feb 21: Modified Hawker Hart K3036, fitted with a Rolls-Royce PV.12 made what was to become the Merlin engine's first flight.

Nov 6: The prototype Hurricane, K5083, had its maiden flight, flown by test pilot 'George' Bulman from Brooklands.

1936
Mar 5: Vickers chief test pilot 'Mutt' Summers carried out the first flight of the Type 300 prototype, K5054, at Eastleigh.

Mar 26: Prototype K5054 delivered to the Aeroplane & Armament Experimental Establishment, Martlesham Heath, for the first of many Air Ministry acceptance trials.

Jun 3: Production contract for 310 Type 300s placed.

1937
Jun 11: Reginald Joseph Mitchell, Supermarine chief designer, died of cancer. Joseph Smith succeeded him and went on to design all the Spitfire variants beyond the Mk.I, the Seafires and the Spiteful and Seafang.

Oct 12: First production Hurricane I, L1547, had its maiden flight, at Brooklands.

Dec: At Northolt, 111 Squadron became the first operational Hurricane unit.

1938
May 14: First Spitfire I, K9787, had its maiden flight at Eastleigh, flown by test pilot Jeffrey Quill.

Jul 12: Construction of the massive Castle Bromwich Air Factory began – see page 52.

Aug 4: First Spitfire I was delivered to an operational unit: K9789 to 19 Squadron at Duxford. (Mk.I K9792 was issued to 19 Squadron on July 27 for initial familiarisation and was ferried to the Central Flying School at Upavon by Jeffrey Quill two days later; it joined 19 Squadron full-time on August 16.) On November 11 the delivery of K9811 brought 19 Squadron up to full strength: 16 aircraft. By then, just over 200 Hurricanes were in squadron service.

Nov 10: The 'High Speed' Spitfire, wearing 'trade plate' markings N17 (RAF serial K9834) was first flown. It was intended for record-breaking, but not used for this purpose.

1939
Feb: Modified Mk.I K9791 began flight testing, serving as the Mk.II prototype.

Sep 1: World War Two started with the German invasion of Poland; Britain declared war on Germany on September 3. At this point, the RAF had nine Spitfire squadrons fully operational: 19 at Duxford, 41 at Catterick, 54 and 65 at Hornchurch, 66 at Duxford, 72 at Church Fenton, 74 at Hornchurch, 602 at Abbotsinch and 611 at Duxford.

Spitfire fuselages at the Itchen works, Southampton, in 1939. In the background is a Supermarine Stranraer flying-boat. ALL KEY COLLECTION UNLESS NOTED

The fifth production Spitfire I, K9791, was used to help develop the Mk.II. On September 25, 1939 Jeffery Quill was testing K9791 when its engine failed at 15,000ft. He made a forced-landing near Weston Zoyland in Somerset and walked away from it. Mk.I K9791 was repaired and went on to join the Photographic Development Unit at Benson in June 1940. PETER GREEN COLLECTION

Spitfire I X4907 was converted to so-called PR.Ig status (later designated PR.VII) and served with 140 Squadron at Benson in early 1942. PETER GREEN COLLECTION

PRE WAR SPITFIRE 'CUSTOMERS'

By 1938 there was a queue of countries clamouring to add Spitfires to their frontline arsenals. As the situation is Europe worsened, it fell to the Air Ministry - itself desperately trying to build squadrons for the RAF - to decide the priorities for the nations that could be allowed to take examples from the Southampton production line. France was given top priority, after which came the following, in order: Belgium*, Estonia, Turkey*, Rumania, Portugal, Switzerland*, Yugoslavia*, Netherlands*, Greece*, Bulgaria and Iran. Those countries marked with an asterisk (*) also requested licence production rights.

Others that made enquiries but did not reach the priority list, for one reason or another, were as follows: China, Egypt, Finland, Japan, Latvia, Lithuania and Poland.

Only two of the 'priority' nations received Spitfires: France took a Mk.I on July 18, 1939 and Turkey received Spitfire I L1066 during September 1939. The US took delivery of Mk.I L1099 in September 1939 for a brief evaluation, before it was flown north for the Canadians to also sample the new fighter.

Beyond the outbreak of World War Two allies and countries of 'special interest' began to receive stocks of Spitfires: Australia (from 1943 in country), Italy (from its abandoning the Rome-Berlin Axis, in 1944); Portugal (from 1942), Soviet Russia (from 1943), Turkey (from 1944) and the United Stated (from 1942).

Sep 6: Following a failure of the nascent radar early warning system, the 'Battle of Barking Creek' showed up flaws in Fighter Command's control system. Airborne units were misidentified; Spitfires of 72 Squadron intercepted and shot down two Hurricanes of 56 Squadron: Plt Off F C Rose survived but tragically Plt Off M Hulton-Harrop was killed in L1985.

Sep 21: Spitfire I L1090 handed over to the United States Army Air Corps at Patterson Field, Dayton, USA for evaluation.

Oct 16: First aircraft shot down in British airspace since 1918: Spitfires of 602 Squadron, based at Drem, shot down two Luftwaffe Junkers Ju 88s, and Spitfires of 603 Squadron, operating from Turnhouse, destroyed a Heinkel He 111. Both enemy aircraft fell into the sea. See October 28.

Oct 28: Following on from the exploits of October 16, Spitfires of 602 and 603 Squadrons brought down an He 111 near Haddington, east of Edinburgh. This was the first enemy aircraft shot down on the British mainland during World War Two.

Nov: Flight trials of the first Spitfire floatplane, L3059, began at the Marine Aircraft Experimental Establishment, Helensburgh.

Nov 22: First operational use of photo-reconnaissance (PR) configured Spitfire, over Luxembourg. Converted during the previous month to interim PR.III status, Mk.I N3071 flew under the guise of the 'Special Survey Flight' from Coulomiers and was piloted by Flt Lt M V 'Shorty' Longbottom.

Nov 30: First Rolls-Royce Griffon engine was ground-run.

1940

Jan 11: Believed to be the first loss of a Spitfire in operations; Mk.I N3036 of 66 Squadron, based at Duxford, was damaged by return fire from a Luftwaffe Heinkel He 111 and was written off in a crash-landing.

Mar 15: Prototype Mk.III, a conversion of Spitfire I N3297, first flown.

May 23: During the campaign running up to Operation Dynamo, the Dunkirk evacuation, Spitfires and Messerschmitt Bf 109s engaged in combat for the first time. Plt Off B H G Learmond of 92 Squadron, forward based at Hornchurch and flying Mk.I P9370, was shot down and killed by a '109 over Dunkirk.

Jun 27: Mk.II P7280, the first to be produced at the Castle Bromwich Aircraft Factory, was issued to service. (See page 52.)

Jul: First Mk.IIs in service, with 152 Squadron at Warmwell.

Jul 10: The 'official' date of the start of the Battle of Britain. A total of 18 Spitfire squadrons were at, or near, readiness: 17 at Hornchurch, 19 at Fowlmere, 41 at Catterick, 54 at Rochford, 64 at Kenley, 65 at Hornchurch, 66 at Coltishall, 72 at Acklington, 92 at Pembrey, 152 at Acklington, 226 at Wittering, 234 at St Eval, 602 at Drem, 603 at Turnhouse, 609 at Middle Wallop, 610 at Biggin Hill, 611 at Digby, 616 at Leconfield. The bulk of the force facing the Luftwaffe was composed of Hurricanes (29 squadrons) plus seven Blenheim and two Defiant squadrons.

Jul 11: First Spitfire pilot to perish during the Battle of Britain was Plt Off G T M Mitchell shot down by Messerschmitt Bf 109s off Portland in Mk.I L1095 of 609 Squadron.

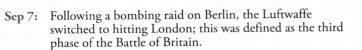
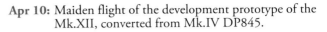

Sep 7: Following a bombing raid on Berlin, the Luftwaffe switched to hitting London; this was defined as the third phase of the Battle of Britain.

Sep 15: The pivotal day of the Battle of Britain, with 56 Luftwaffe aircraft downed. The date has since been named 'Battle of Britain Day'.

Oct 31: The month of October 1940 was defined as the fourth and last phase of the Battle of Britain.

Dec 26: Prototype Mk.V, a conversion of Mk.I N9788, first flown.

1941

Feb: First Mk.Vs in service, with 92 Squadron at Biggin Hill.

May 21: Plt Off M Suckling of the Photographic Reconnaissance Unit flew from Wick in Scotland to the Norwegian coast in a Spitfire and brought back images of the battleship *Bismarck* anchored at Bergen. This sparked the massive operation that resulted in the vessel's sinking.

Jun 26: Prototype Mk.VI, a conversion of Mk.I X4942, first flown.

Jul 18: First Spitfire, a Mk.I, built by Westland at Yeovil, was delivered to service. Westland built 685 Mk.Is and Mk.Vs, followed by 2,115 Seafires – see also October 12, 1946.

Sep 20: Converted Mk.III N3297 first flown at Hucknall as the development prototype of Mk.IX.

Oct: First 'hooked' Spitfire, Mk.V BL676, started trials – the beginning of the Seafire family. See also March 23, 1942.

Nov 27: Prototype Mk.IV, DP845, first Spitfire with a Griffon engine, had its maiden flight.

1942

Feb: Spitfire V AD371, converted to the Seafire II series prototype, began flight testing.

Mar 7: First unit-strength deployment overseas: Mk.Vs reached Malta courtesy of the USS *Wasp*. Spitfires launched from its deck flew the final 400 miles (643km) to the island.

Mar 23: Spitfire V BL676 (see October 1941), re-engineered as the first 'true' Seafire I MB328, was first flown.

Apr: First Mk.VIs in service, with 616 Squadron at Kings Cliffe.

Apr: Mk.V AB450, converted to Mk.VII status, started testing as the variant development prototype.

Apr 10: Maiden flight of the development prototype of the Mk.XII, converted from Mk.IV DP845.

May 25: First successful high-altitude interception by a pressurised Spitfire VI; taking down a Dornier Do 217 on a sortie out of Kings Cliffe.

Jun: At Atcham in Shropshire, members of the 31st Fighter Group, USAAF, accepted the first operational Spitfires to serve with the American forces.

Jul: First Mk.IXs entered service, with 64 Squadron at Hornchurch.

Jul 30: A Focke-Wulf Fw 190 fell to the guns of Flt Lt Don Kingaby of 64 Squadron, based at Hornchurch – the first victory for the Spitfire IX.

Aug 17: Twelve Boeing B-17E Fortresses of the USAAF 97th Bomb Group were escorted by RAF Spitfires on the 'Mighty Eighth's' inaugural mission, to Rouen, France.

Aug 24: Flying a specially 'tweaked' Spitfire V, Fg Off G W H Reynolds climbed to 42,000ft (12,800m) and intercepted a Junkers Ju 86P on a reconnaissance sortie over Alexandria, Egypt.

Sep: First Mk.VIIs entered service, with the High Altitude Flight at Northolt. Initial 'full' unit was 124 Squadron at North Weald in March 1943.

Sep 29: The American-manned RAF 'Eagle' Squadrons, 71, 121 and 133, were officially transferred to the USAAF to form respectively the 334th, 335th and 336th Fighter Squadrons of the 4th Fighter Group.

Oct 4: Flight trials of converted Mk.IV (also known as Mk.XX) DP851 started, testing the new wing destined for the Mk.21.

Nov 9: Prototype Seafire III, converted from Mk.II MA9770, first flown.

Nov 20: First production Mk.VIII, JF274, had its maiden flight.

Dec: PR.XIs entered service, with 541 Squadron at Benson. ➽

In October 1939 the Spitfire Is of 610 Squadron became operational at Wittering. The unit flew Spitfires until July 1951 when it traded its F.22s for Gloster Meteor jets.

COMMONWEALTH AND OVERSEAS RAF AND FAA SPITFIRE SQUADRONS

Nation	Sqn	From	To	Variants*
Australia	451	Feb 1943	Jan 1946	V, IX, XVI, XIV
	452	Apr 1941	Jun 1942	I, II, V
	453	Jun 1942	Jan 1946	I, V, IX, XVI
	457	Jun 1941	Jun 1942	I, II, V
Belgium	349	Jun 1943	Oct 1946	V, IX, XVI
	350	Nov 1941	Oct 1946	II, V, IX, XIV, XVI
Canada	400	Dec 1943	Apr 1945	XI, XIII
	401	Sep 1941	Jun 1945	II, V, IX, XIV
	402	Mar 1942	Jul 1945	V, IX, XIV, XVI
	403	May 1941	Jun 1945	I, II, V, IX, XVI
	411	Jun 1941	Mar 1946	I, II, V, IX, XIV, XVI
	412	Jul 1941	Mar 1946	II, V, IX, XIV, XVI
	414	Jul 1944	Aug 1945	V, IX, XIV
	416	Nov 1941	Mar 1946	II, V, IX, XIV, XVI
	417	Nov 1941	Jun 1945	II, V, VIII, IX
	421	Apr 1942	Jul 1945	V, IX, XVI
	430	Nov 1944	Aug 1945	XIV
	441	Feb 1944	Jun 1945	V, IX
	442	Feb 1944	May 1945	V, IX
	443	Feb 1944	Mar 1946	V, IX, XIV, XVI
	803	Aug 1945	Jan 1946	Seafire XV [1]
	883	Nov 1945	Nov 1948	Seafire XV [1]
Czechoslovakia	310	Oct 1941	Feb 1946	II, V, IX
	312	Oct 1941	Feb 1946	II, V, IX
	313	Mar 1941	Feb 1946	I, II, V, VI, VII, IX
France	326	Dec 1943	Nov 1945	V, IX
	327	Dec 1943	Nov 1945	V, VIII, IX
	328	Dec 1943	Nov 1945	V, VIII, IX
	329	Feb 1944	Nov 1945	V, IX, XVI
	340	Nov 1941	Nov 1945	II, V, IX, XVI
	341	Jan 1943	Nov 1945	V, IX, XVI
	345	Mar 1944	Nov 1945	V, IX, XVI
Greece	335	Dec 1943	Jul 1946	V
	336	Jul 1944	Jul 1946	V
India	8	Jul 1944	May 1947	VIII, XIV
	9	May 1945	Jun 1946	VIII, XIV
	10	Jul 1945	May 1947	VIII
Netherlands	167	Oct 1942	Jun 1943	V
	322	Jun 1943	Oct 1945	IX, XIV, XVI
New Zealand	485	Mar 1941	Aug 1945	I, II, V, IX, XVI
Norway	331	Nov 1941	Nov 1945	II, V, IX
	332	Jan 1942	Sep 1945	V, IX
Poland	302	Oct 1941	Dec 1946	V, IX, XVI
	303	Jan 1941	Apr 1945	I, II, V, IX
	306	Jul 1941	Mar 1943	II, V, IX
	308	Apr 1941	Dec 1946	I, II, V, IX, XVI
	315	Jul 1941	Mar 1944	II, V, IX
	316	Oct 1941	Apr 1944	V, IX
	317	Oct 1941	Dec 1946	V, IX, XVI
	318	Feb 1944	Aug 1946	V, IX
South Africa	1	Nov 1942	Oct 1943	V, VIII, IX
	2	Jul 1943	Jul 1945	V, IX
	3	Mar 1944	Oct 1945	V, IX
	4	Jul 1943	Jul 1945	V, IX
	7	Jul 1943	Jul 1945	V, IX
	9	Jun 1944	Feb 1945	V, IX
	10	Jul 1944	Oct 1945	V, IX
	40	Feb 1943	Oct 1945	V, IX, XI
	41	Feb 1944	Nov 1944	V, IX
Southern Rhodesia	237	Dec 1943	Dec 1945	V, IX
USA	71	Aug 1941	Sep 1942	II, V [2]
	121	Oct 1941	Sep 1942	II, V [2]
	133	Oct 1941	Sep 1942	II, V [2]
Yugoslavia	352	Jun 1944	Jun 1945	V

Notes: * Main variants only; not necessarily presented in chronological order of service. [1] Fleet Air Arm units. [2] American-manned, but non-allied, 'Eagle' Squadrons; re-formed on September 29, 1942 as fully fledged USAAF units, respectively: 334th, 335th and 336th Fighter Squadrons, 4th Fighter Group.

Named 'Bombay City' in honour of the Indian Spitfire Fund, Mk.V BM252 first served with 122 Squadron at Hornchurch in May 1942. KEC

1943

Feb: At Darwin, Australia, 54 Squadron RAF became operational – first use of Spitfires in the Pacific theatre.

Feb: First Mk.XIIs in service, with 41 Squadron at Llanbedr.

Mar: Converted Mk.I L1004, first flown on initial trials for Mk.XIII.

Apr: PR.XIIIs entered service, with 542 Squadron at Benson.

Jul: First Mk.VIIIs in service, with 145 Squadron on Sicily, Italy.

Aug: Mk.21 PP139, the first production example, began flight trials.

Sep: Converted Mk.VIII JG204, started flight testing as the F.23 developmental prototype.

Sep 7: Mk.VIII JF317 first flown in the guise of the Mk.XIV developmental prototype.

Oct: Based in eastern India, 136, 607 and 615 Squadrons, all equipped with Mk.Vs, were declared operational in the India-Burma theatre.

Mk.IX MJ892 was converted to a floatplane, making its first flight at Beaumaris, Anglesey, in July 1944.

A Spitfire unleashing its fire power against the gun butts.

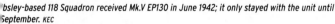

Ibsley-based 118 Squadron received Mk.V EP130 in June 1942; it only stayed with the unit until September. KEC

Spitfire XII MB878 was used for trials with a 500lb bomb under its centre section at Boscombe Down from September 1943.

Oct: Converted Mk.IX MH850 was first flown as the developmental prototype for the Mk.XVI.

Nov: Prototype Seafire XV, NS487, first flown.

Nov 8: Based at Chittagong, India, Spitfire Vs of 615 Squadron shot down a Japanese Mitsubishi Ki-46 *Dinah* – the type's initial success in the Burma theatre.

1944

The ever-increasing number of Spitfire designations forced a re-think in 1944. Roman numerals (eg Mk.XVI) continued but once Mk.XX had been reached, the change was made to Arabic, hence Spitfire Mk.21 etc. In 1948 the decision was taken to adopt Arabic numerals throughout. For example, Spitfire PR.XIXs became PR.19s.

Jan: First Mk.XIVs entered service, with 610 Squadron at Exeter.

Feb: First Seafire IIIs in service, with 899 Squadron.

Mar 15: Prototype F.21, LA187, had its maiden flight.

Apr 4: Mk.X prototype, MD192, first flown.

Jun: Prototype Seafire XVII, converted from Mk.XV NS493, begins flight test.

Jun 6: On the morning of the D-Day invasion Fg Off Johnnie' Houlton of 485 Squadron Royal New Zealand Air Force shot down a Junkers Ju 88 – it was the first of many enemy aircraft dispatched that day. 'Kiwi' Houlton was flying Spitfire IX ML407, which is still in fine form – see page 50.

Jun 23: Flying a Spitfire XIV out of West Malling, Fg Off K R Collier was the first to 'flip' a V-1 flying-bomb. Frustrated that he had expended his ammunition, he flew alongside the 'Doodlebug' and used his wing tip to topple it, causing its gyros to fail so that it plummeted to the ground.

Jun: Developmental prototype for the Spiteful, NN660, was first flown by Jeffrey Quill.

Sep: Converted Spitfire F.21 TM379 completed as the prototype Seafire F.45, began tests during the month, and similarly re-configured F.21 TM383 started trials as the Seafire F.46 prototype, on the 8th. ➲

All over Great Britain, across the Commonwealth and worldwide, cities, towns and organisations raised money for the 'Spitfire Fund' to 'buy' one of the fighters for the war effort. This poster features the ninth Mk.I K9795 which was issued to 19 Squadron at Duxford on September 27, 1938.

OVERSEAS OPERATORS

Spitfire V EP210 was shipped to the Soviet Union in October 1942.

Air Arm	From	To	Main variants
South African Air Force	Nov 1942	Apr 1954	V, IX
Royal Australian Air Force	Feb 1943	Aug 1945	II, V, VIII
Belgian Air Force	Oct 1946	Oct 1954	IX, XIV, XVI
Union of Burma Air Force	Apr 1948	1954	IX, XVIII, Seafire XV
Royal Canadian Air Force	Apr 1941	Mar 1946	II, V, IX, XIV, XVI
Royal Canadian Navy	Jun 1946	Dec 1948	Seafire XV
Czechoslovakian Air Force	Aug 1945	1948	IX
Danish Air Force	Aug 1947	Jun 1955	IX, XI
Danish Naval Air Service	Aug 1947	1951	IX, XI
Royal Egyptian Air Force [1]	Feb 1945	1956	V, IX, Tr.IX, F.22
French Air Force	Jan 1945	Dec 1953	I, V, VIII, IX
French Naval Air Arm	Mar 1946	May 1953	IX, Seafire III, XV
Royal Hellenic Air Force	Apr 1946	Jul 1954	V, IX
Royal Hong Kong Aux Air Force	Apr 1952	1955	XIX, F.24
Royal Indian Air Force [2]	Jul 1944	Jul 1958	VIII, Tr.IX, XI, XIV, XVIII, XIX
Irish Air Corps	Feb 1947	1960	Tr.IX, Seafire IIII
Israel Defence Force / Air Force	Sep 1948	Oct 1956	IX
Italian Air Force	Sep 1944	1952	V, IX
Netherlands Air Force	May 1946	Sep 1953	IX, Tr.IX
Royal Norwegian Air Force	May 1945	Aug 1953	IX, XI
Portuguese Air Force	Nov 1942	Jan 1948	I, V
Southern Rhodesian Air Force	Mar 1951	1954	F.22
Singapore Fighter Squadron [3]	May 1951	Feb 1954	XVIII, F.24
Soviet (Russian) Air Force	Jan 1943	c1951	IV, V, IX
Royal Swedish Air Force	Jan 1949	Aug 1955	XIX
Syrian Air Force	May 1954	c1959	F.22
Royal Thai Air Force	Dec 1950	Apr 1955	XIV, XIX
Turkish Air Force	Sep 1939	1954	I, V, IX, XIX
United States Army Air Force	Sep 1942	mid-1945	I, V, VIII, IX, XI
United States Navy	Feb 1944	1945	V, Seafire II
Yugoslavian Air Force	Jun 1945	1952	V, IX

Notes: See also page 60. [1] Egyptian Air Force from July 1953. [2] Indian Air Force from December 1949. [3] Part of Malayan Auxiliary Air Force. Compiled with frequent reference to *Spitfire International* by Helmut Terbeck, Harry van der Meer and Ray Sturtivant, Air-Britain, 2002.

Boasting a shark's mouth and a 'slipper' fuel tank, a Spitfire VIII of 457 Squadron Royal Australian Air Force at Morotai in February 1945.

Mk.VIII JF447 carrying the winged sword of 601 Squadron on its fin. This machine joined the unit in Italy in November 1943.

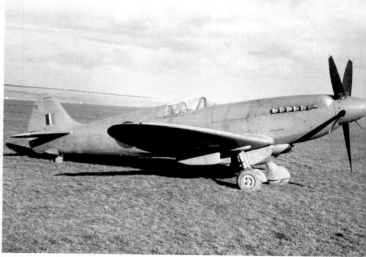

The prototype PR.XIX, SW777, was first flown by 'Pat' Shea-Simmonds in October 1944. KEC

Proudly carrying the red and white chequer markings of Poland, Mk.IX MH869 of Northolt-based 302 'Poznanski' Squadron, late 1943.

Seafire II touching down on the deck of a carrier. FLEET AIR ARM MUSEUM

Mk.VIII JF321 was converted in August 1943 as a development prototype for the Mk.XIV. Test flying included a Rotol contra-rotating airscrew.

Oct: Prototype PR.XIX SW777 first flown.

Oct 5: Spitfire IXs of 401 Squadron, Royal Canadian Air Force, based in the Netherlands, shot down a Messerschmitt Me 262 – the first time the twin-jet had been destroyed in the air.

Nov: First PR.XIXs in service, with 542 Squadron at Benson.

Nov: Coltishall-based 602 Squadron put first Mk.XVIs into service.

Nov: Prototype F.22, SX549, began flight testing.

Dec 30: Three Focke-Wulf Fw 190s and a pair of Messerschmitt Bf 109s were shot down in one sortie by Flt Lt R J Audet of 411 Squadron, Royal Canadian Air Force, flying a Spitfire IX. Operating from Heesch in the Netherlands, Audet became the only 'ace in a day' Spitfire pilot.

1945

Jan: F.21s entered service, with 91 Squadron at Manston.

Apr 24: Spitfire V AB910 flew a 'passenger' – see page 30.

Jul 6: First production MK.XVIII, SM843, had its inaugural flight.

Sep: Seafire XVs went into service for the first time, with 883 Squadron.

Nov 30: Last Spitfire built at Castle Bromwich, Mk.22 PK614, had its maiden flight. Production of fuselages and sub-assemblies continued into 1946.

1946

Feb: First production Mk.24, PK678, had its maiden flight.

Apr 25: Prototype Seafire F.47 PS845 first flown.

Jun 18: 'True' prototype of the Seafang, F.32 VB895, first flown.

Aug: Mk.XVIIIs entered service, with 208 Squadron at Ein Shemer, Palestine. (See page 66.)

Sep 9: Prototype Tr.VIII two-seater, converted from Mk.VIII MT818, first flown, see page 50.

TAIL HEAVY

Spitfire V AB910 carried a 'passenger' in April 1945. It went on to join the Battle of Britain Memorial Flight and is seen in the foreground of an incredible formation staged in November 1973. Behind AB910 are: Mk.II P7350, Hurricane PZ865, Hurricane LF363, Spitfire XIX PM631 and Spitfire XIX PS853. KEC

To help keep the tail down when taxying out for take-off in blustery conditions, groundcrew frequently sat on the leading edge of the tailplane and took a (draughty) ride. While serving with 53 Operational Conversion Unit at Hibaldstow, Flt Lt Neil Cox DFC*, piloting Mk.V AB910, forgot a pre-flight check item. He hit the throttle before WAAF LAC Margaret Horton could 'dismount'. She flung herself across the fin and held on for all she was worth. Cox soon appreciated that his spitfire was tail heavy and the elevator was not responsive. A gentle circuit brought Spitfire and 'passenger' safely back to terra firma. Castle Bromwich-built AB910 is still with us; part of the Battle of Britain Memorial Flight.

Oct 12: Last Westland-built Seafire, a Mk.XVII, delivered to service. This completed production of Spitfires and Seafires at Yeovil.

1947
Jan 1: Four Mk.XVIIIs of 60 Squadron attacked communist forces at Kota Tinggi in Johore, Malaya. This was the last time that RAF Spitfires expended weaponry in operational service.

1948
Jul 6: Two Spitfire XVIIIs of 60 Squadron attacked communist insurgents at Ayer Karah in Perak, Malaya, with cannon fire and rocket projectiles. This was a brief operational era for Spitfires as they were replaced by Bristol Beaufighters in the ground attack role the following month.

1954
Apr 1: Last operational flight by a Spitfire, staged by 81 Squadron at Seletar, Singapore, by PR.XIX PS888 and to prove it, the name *The Last* was painted on the cowling.

1957
Jun 10: Last sortie by a civilian-operated Spitfire PR.XIX of the RAF Temperature and Humidity Flight, at Woodvale. This was the final tasking by a Spitfire wearing RAF roundels, see page 88. The Spitfire was PS853 which is still airworthy, see page 86.

1958
May 21: Battle of Britain Flight formed at Biggin Hill. On June 1, 1969 it was re-named as the present-day Battle of Britain Memorial Flight. (See page 88.)

Jul: The Indian Air Force withdrew its last operational Spitfires, PR.XIXs. These *could* well have been the last frontline examples; although that accolade could go to Syria, which *may* have been flying F.22s into 1959. ●

Royal Netherlands Air Force Spitfire Tr.9 H-99 (previously Mk.IX BS147) was handed over in March 1948.

FREEDOM FIGHTERS

**Sleek, swift, manoeuvrable, strong and well-constructed.
Philosophy Football's commemorative T-shirt pays tribute to the Spitfire
as the defender of our freedom from Nazism.**

MASS PRODUCED
ADAPTABLE

Rolls-Royce continued to increase the power on the Merlin and the Mk.V basked in the 40- and 50-series engines, initially offering a hefty 1,440hp. Armament options caused production problems, eight 0.303in machine guns or two 20mm cannon and four '303s'.

SPITFIRE V FACTFILE

The first production Spitfire Vc, AA873, was a 'presentation' machine, having been subscribed to by the Manchester Air Cadets – although the script lettering under the canopy actually had the last word reading 'Cadd' by the time this image was taken at Boscombe Down in January 1942. KEY COLLECTION

Engine:	Rolls-Royce Merlin 45, 46, 50, 55 or 56 – Merlin 45 rated at 1,440hp (1,074kW)
Statistics:	Dimensions: Span 36ft 10in (11.23m) Length 32ft 2in (9.8m) Height 29ft 11in (9.12m)
	Weights: (Mk.Va) Empty 4,981lb (2,259kg) Loaded 6,070lb (2,753kg) Performance: (Mk. Va) Max speed 368mph (593km/h) Service ceiling 38,000ft (11,582m)
Armament:	Mk.Va eight 0.303in machine guns; Mk.Vb two 20mm cannon, plus four 0.303in machine guns; Mk.Vc with the 'universal wing' with options of eight machine guns, two cannons and four machine guns, or four cannon
First flown:	December 26, 1940, Mk.I K9788 fitted with Merlin XX, effectively the Mk.V prototype
Number built:	6,787 (some say 6,465) by Supermarine, Castle Bromwich and Westland
Sub-Variants:	Mk.Va, Mk.Vb and Mk.Vc armament options. Tropical conversions with filter and later so-called 'Aboukir' filter, known as, eg Mk.Vb(Trop). Conversions to tactical reconnaissance as FR.V and floatplane. One known two-seater, in-field conversion by 4 Squadron, SAAF, 1943.

DAY FIGHTER

With the introduction of the Mk.Vc and the 'universal wing', [tha]t that could be adapted to either [o]ption, or four 20mm cannon. [W]hile designed for air defence, it [w]as also capable of taking a long- [r]ange tank or a 500lb (226kg) [u]nder the centre section, or a pair [o]f 250-pounders, one under each wing. An air filter housed in an ugly-looking fairing under the nose facilitated operation in Middle East, Far East and Pacific theatres.

At Biggin Hill, 92 Squadron took delivery of the first Mk.Vs in February 1941. The final Mk.Vs were produced in the late summer of 1943.

Below
Built at Castle Bromwich, Mk.Vc JG891 was transferred to the RAAF as A58-178 in February 1943. It crash-landed in Papua New Guinea in January 1944 and there the hulk lingered until it was salvaged in 1974. Brought to Duxford in 1999 it was lovingly restored and appeared in RAF colours with desert camouflage and air filter, making its first flight on November 2, 2006. It carried the initials of its owner, Tom Blair and was dispatched to its new home in the USA in 2008.
JOHN M DIBBS – PLANE PICTURE COMPANY

RHODES EAGLES

Commonwealth countries made a huge contribution to the RAF's operations during World War Two. Among them was 266 Squadron, the only Rhodesian-manned unit in Fighter Command, which established a fine reputation in the skies over Western Europe.

Formed on October 30, 1939, Spitfire Is arrived in early 1940 to replace 266's interim Fairey Battles. It became operational in May and was in action over the Dunkirk beaches on June 2, 1940. Moving south 266 saw action in the Battle of Britain during August when in little more than a week it claimed nine destroyed, six 'probables' and 11 damaged for the loss of six pilots killed and five wounded.

On August 21, the unit moved to Wittering to rest and reform. Through the autumn and early winter months 266 maintained readiness. It flew sector patrols and convoy escorts into 1941.

INTO THE NIGHT

The New Year began with a heavy snowfall at Wittering but that afternoon Plt Off Gosling in Spitfire I X4646 scrambled to intercept a 'plot' and orbited Boston in the unit's first sortie of 191. More significantly, on January 1 it was announced that Rhodesians would begin to be posted in, and that it would be retitled as 266 (Rhodesia) Squadron, although this was not officially achieved until August 1941.

New Zealander Sqn Ldr 'Jamie' Jameson was 266's CO and through the early winter months the unit continued sector patrols and convoy escorts, often in the face of unfavourable weather.

During one patrol, on the morning of March 8, Sgt John von Schaick claimed 266's first success of the year. Flying Spitfire I X4164 he shot down Junkers Ju 88A-5 0404 'F6+BM', flown by Ofw Beuker

off Skegness. Sadly, von Schaick's wingman, Plt Off 'Freddie' Ferris, was hit by return fire and lost.

To enable 266 Squadron to fly defence sorties to counter the night Blitz, training in nocturnal sorties, known as 'Fighter Nights' began. Success was not far off, on April 8/9 during a patrol over Coventry, the CO spotted a Heinkel He 111 against the moon and shot it down this was no mean feat in a single-seat day fighter! The next night Flt Lt Armitage almost repeated the feat but could only claim a probable.

BIRTHDAY PARTY

Offensive sweeps over northern France began on an April 15, along with 65 Squadron and the Canadian 402 Squadron, 266 was involved in a costly sortie. It ran into German 'ace' Obst Lt Adolf Galland who was on his way to a birthday party at Le Touquet with his Messerschmitt Bf 109F laden with lobster and

A'S

ANDREW THOMAS OUTLINES THE EXPLOITS OF
THE RHODESIAN-MANNED 266 SQUADRON

champagne. Conducting a small diversion, he engaged 266's Spitfires and forced down three to crash-landings.

The first Rhodesian had arrived the previous day when Plt Off 'Colly' Collcutt took over as adjutant, followed by the first pilot Sgt Cyril Whiteford, three days later: Whiteford flew his first 'op' on May 5. Six more Rhodesians followed: Fg Off Charles Green, Plt Offs Allen Allen-White, Hugh Parry and 'Zulu' Buchanan, and Sgts Gordon Williams and P Devenish.

Fighter Nights were still flown, with conspicuous success coming during a raid on London on May 10/11 when Jamieson found a He 111 silhouetted against the flames, bringing the raider down near Romford. Plt Off Andrew Humphrey chased another Heinkel as far as Rotterdam where he shot it down, then promptly destroyed a second.

Left
Sqn Ldr Charles Green (centre) was 266's first Rhodesian CO. With him are his two Rhodesian Flight Commanders, Flt Lt Rolo Dawson (right) who claimed its penultimate Spitfire victory, and Flt Lt A C Johnston (left) who claimed the last! P COOKE

Below
Spitfire I X4646 flew 266 Squadron's first sortie of 1941 with Plt Off Gosling at the controls. RAF WITTERING RECORDS

Above
Sgt Johnny Plagis joined 266 Squadron in July 1941 and became the most successful Rhodesian pilot of World War Two.
VIA C F SHORES

Above right
Sgt Ian Munro shared in the destruction of a He 111 to claim the first victory by a 266 Squadron Rhodesian. P COOKE

Right
Sgt Bob Sergeant on the wing of his 266 Squadron Spitfire.
AUTHOR'S COLLECTION

"THEY RAN INTO GERMAN 'ACE' ADOLF GALLAND WHO WAS ON HIS WAY TO A BIRTHDAY PARTY AT LE TOUQUET WITH HIS BF 109F LADEN WITH LOBSTER AND CHAMPAGNE."

Lewis destroyed a Bf 109 but Plt Offs Cook and Holland were lost.

The first blooding for the Rhodesians came during a sweep with 257 and 401 Squadrons over Northern France on the afternoon of July 3. Taking off at 14:45 the French coast was crossed near Boulogne. Approaching Hazebrouck at 16:00 around 50 Bf 109s were encountered and a whirling dogfight ensued.

Plt Off Allen-White's Spitfire was hit by cannon fire, but he turned the tables and managed to hit his assailant. Flying P8566, Gordon Matthews, aged 20, became the first Rhodesian lost with 266. Plt Off Gordon Barraclough immediately shot down Matthews' assailant.

During this first operation as a 'Rhodesian' squadron the CO, Sqn Ldr Beresford, was also successful as he described: "I singled out ...one which was lagging and got onto his tail. I gave him a five-second burst from 200 yards closing to 100 yards and saw him dive vertically down smoking. Sgt Devenish saw this aircraft hit the ground.

"Later I saw three Me 109s 2,000ft above turning sharply to port. The first two peeled off and attacked Black Section, who were behind me, the third aircraft continued to climb and turn until it stalled. I was able to close during his climb to about 70 yards and held him in my sights for

In early June, the CO, Sqn Ldr Jameson, was posted to be the Wittering Wing Leader. He remarked: "There was a great spirit in 266 and I was sad to have to hand over direct command..."

RHODESIAN-MANNED
Sqn Ldr Barne Beresford took over as the numbers of Rhodesians

increased. Many scrambles were uneventful such as on the evening of June 12 when Sgt Eric Dicks-Sherwood in P8167 climbed to 18,000ft (5,486m) above cloud but was then ordered to return to base.

The first 'Circus' a large-scale fighter and bomber operation intended to bring up enemy fighters for 266 took place on June 27. Sgt

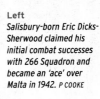

FIRST CLAIM

By early August, more Rhodesians arrived: Sgts Victor Carne, George Elcombe, Reg Hardy, Ian Munro, Johnny Plagis, Wilf Smithyman and Alistair Spence-Ross. This meant that 266 was almost completely Rhodesian manned. Plagis flew his first operational sortie on the 25th and was to end with 17 victories as the most successful Rhodesian pilot of the war.

Flt Lt Desmond McMullen, a very successful RAF pilot was also posted in as a flight commander and he was soon in action with his new unit. During a convoy patrol on August 19 he was leading one of the new Rhodesians, Munro, when they encountered a He 111 during a shipping protection patrol. They made repeated attacks from different angles and eventually the Heinkel dropped its nose and went into the sea; there were no survivors. Munro's claim was the first confirmed victory by a Rhodesian pilot on the unit.

The following day the unit officially became 266 (Rhodesia) Squadron. In December, the squadron badge was officially presented by the High Commissioner for Southern Rhodesia. The badge depicted a Rhodesian Bataleur eagle with the motto 'Hlabezulu' translating as 'Stabber in the Sky'.

Offensive work predominated,

a three-second burst. He dropped away from his stall and spun towards the ground. In view of the fact that we were 40 miles in France and other aircraft were about it was impossible to watch longer."

During the fight, Sgt Cyril Whitehead engaged two Bf 109s, probably destroying one and damaging the other, to register the first claims by a Rhodesian pilot in the unit.

typical being a Rhubarb harassing operation by Wg Cdr Jameson and Plt Off Hugh Parry on September 10 when they attacked and damaged a 1,000-ton ship off Holland. Two days later Parry destroyed a Bf l09, again off the Dutch coast. It was on that day that Sgt Johnny Deall – a future ace – arrived.

WHIRLING DOGFIGHT

At 15:00 on the afternoon of September 15, 1941 a pair of 266's Spitfires flown by Wg Cdr Jameson and Sgt Dicks-Sherwood left Coltishall for a strike on the northern Dutch coast port of de Kooy. Jameson was in P8509, which was named *The Old Lady*, having been presented by the staff of the Bank of England, which is nicknamed 'The Old Lady of Threadneedle Street'. Dicks-Sherwood was also flying in a presentation aircraft P8505, a gift from the people of Stamford, Lincolnshire.

Jameson described the afternoon's events when they encountered Bf 110s from II/ZG 26: "We flew just below the cloud base, which was at about 2,500ft, and in a wide line abreast. When we were about 40 miles from the Dutch coast, Sherwood ➔

suddenly shouted 'Aircraft astern', and turned hard to port. Immediately I too turned steeply to port and saw four Messerschmitt 110s, the leading one being only 400 yards from me. We had been very close to getting 'bounced'.

"Now our two Spitfires were almost head-on to the enemy, with a closing speed of around 600mph, and both sides were firing. Fire from the leading enemy went under my starboard wing, while the second's all passed below. None of my shots seemed to strike home.

"It quickly became a whirling dogfight. Sherwood manoeuvred valiantly, getting in another head-on attack, during which there was a large flash in the cockpit of the enemy aircraft, but another was almost on his tail. I had seen the danger, however, and was desperately trying to get my sights on the Me 110.

"Just as it opened fire, scoring hits on Sherwood's machine, I pressed the gun button, firing a two-second burst from 150 yards. This was lethal. The Me dropped a wing and plunged straight into the sea. Sherwood, meanwhile, broke away and wisely used cloud cover."

The veteran Jameson had achieved his fifth victory in the Spitfire. For the 24-year-old Dicks-Sherwood the 'damaged' was his first claim; he became an ace over Malta the following year.

CANNON PUNCH

By this time, the latest enemy fighters outclassed 266's Spitfire IIs. It was with some relief that later in September, after moving to Martlesham Heath, the unit re-equipped with the cannon-armed Spitfire Vb.

In early October 1941, 266 moved to Wittering's satellite at Collyweston from where it resumed operations. The first Spitfire V victory occurred on the 13th when Flt Lt McMullen destroyed a Bf 109 during a 'Circus' and Flt Lt Green damaged another.

A few days later, Green was promoted to become 266's first Rhodesian CO and he celebrated the event within the week by sharing with Dicks-Sherwood the destruction of a Dornier Do 217 off Cromer. This was the first confirmed victory for each of them.

They had spotted the Dornier flying at about 500ft, some 1,000

yards away, and Green attacked first, his burst causing an explosion in the starboard engine. The bomber dived in an attempt to escape, but a second burst set the fuselage on fire and it cartwheeled into the sea. It was 266's last victory of the year.

FRUSTRATING TYPHOON

On January 6, 1942 the first example of the RAF's latest fighter, the Typhoon, arrived for 266. Teething troubles meant that the conversion was a slow process so operations continued on Spitfires.

The unit diary recalled a sortie on the 11th: "Three aircraft on a convoy patrol took off from Docking having heard that enemy aircraft might be expected. When near the convoy's position, told of enemy aircraft [e/a] approaching – then saw a Ju 88 and chased it in line.

"Closing to 200 yards, Plt Off Small opened fire as the e/a crossed 100 yards in front of him and continued firing following the e/a into cloud. On emerging from cloud, Small and Sgt Norham Lucas rejoined and tried to call Flt Lt Allen-White on R/T, but without success. Allen-White is missing."

By the end of January, 266 had

seven Typhoons on strength and continued a somewhat mixed existence with 'B' Flight converting at Duxford while 'A' Flight was detached to Coltishall for operations.

The CO worked hard to get 266 ready on the new type but it was a frustrating experience. 'A' Flight remained active, seeing some inconclusive action during the 'Channel Dash' on February 12. Ten Spitfires from Coltishall scrambled to cover the withdrawal of bombers that attacked the German warships sailing through the Channel.

While on a dusk convoy patrol in a Spitfire on the 24th, Plt Off Rolo Dawson spotted four Do 217s at wave-top height and he shot one down. Dawson recalled: "The Dornier jettisoned his bomb load and made off, skimming low over the waves. I gave chase and opened fire. In no time the 'Hun' was thoroughly on fire. Then he heeled over and dived into the sea leaving a great patch of burning wreckage and oil."

Spitfire operations gradually reduced and 266 claimed its final scalp on the Supermarine fighter on April 29. Off Yarmouth Flt Lt A C Johnston shot down a Ju 88 into the sea to close an incredible era for Rhodesia's Eagles.

"GREEN ATTACKED FIRST, HIS BURST CAUSING AN EXPLOSION IN THE STARBOARD ENGINE. THE BOMBER DIVED IN AN ATTEMPT TO ESCAPE BUT A SECOND BURST SET THE FUSELAGE ON FIRE AND IT CARTWHEELED INTO THE SEA."

Supermarine Spitfire *80* MK.VIII

FOCKE-WULF FW 190
ADVERSARY

Spitfire Vs were more than up to the challenge of Messerschmitt Bf 109s, but the Focke-Wulf Fw 190 – nicknamed the 'Butcher Bird' – was another matter. A new version of the Spitfire was needed to counter the powerful, radial-engined Luftwaffe fighter and Rolls-Royce set to developing a Merlin fitted with a two-stage turbocharger – the Series 61.

The definitive counterpoint to the Fw 190 was the Mk.VIII, but it was leap-frogged by the Mk.IX (see page 48). The Mk.IX first flew more than a year before the Mk.VIII because it was based on the well-proven and industry-honed Mk.V. When definitive Mk.VIII

SPITFIRE VIII FACTFILE

Engine:	Rolls-Royce Merlin 61, 63, 66 or 70 – LF.VIII Merlin 66 rated at 1,580hp (1,170kW)
Statistics:	Dimensions: (LF.VIII) Span 32ft 2in (9.80m) Length 30ft 4in (9.25m) Weights: Empty 5,805lb (2,633kg) Loaded 7,807lb (3,541kg) Performance: Max speed 408mph (657km/h) Service ceiling 43,000ft (13,106m)
Armament:	Four 0.303in machine guns and two 20mm cannon
First flown:	November 20, 1942, first production example, JF274
Number built:	1,654 by Supermarine
Sub-Variants:	F, LF and HF versions. Single Tr.8 two-seater converted post-war - see page 82.

Initially delivered to the Air Fighting Development Unit at Wittering in August 1943, Mk.VIII JF299 was transferred to Boscombe Down the following month. There it was used for trials with a 'low-back' rear fuselage and a teardrop canopy. The tropical filter was later replaced. KEY COLLECTION

JF247 had its maiden flight, on November 20, 1942, it was clearly a much more refined development, including such finesse as a retractable tailwheel. (Tucking the tailwheel away may have marginally improved the performance, but many ground crew – wartime and present-day – would claim that it was a complication too far!)

On Sicily in June 1943, it fell to 145 Squadron to inaugurate the Mk.VIII into operations and it quickly gained a reputation as a superb fighting machine, although it was always to be in the shadow of the more prolific 'half-way house', the Mk.IX. Production of the Mk.VIII was complete by the winter of 1944.

Below
Intended for the RAF as MV154, this Spitfire VIII was diverted for service with the RAAF, as A58-671 and was accepted for service in December 1944. De-mobbed in late 1948 it became an instructional airframe in Sydney before passing into the hands of several private owners from 1961. Shipped to the UK in 1979, the Mk.VIII began restoration to flying condition at Duxford for well-known pilot and operator Robs Lamplough. The work was completed at Filton, Bristol, and – as G-BKMI – in May 1994. It was painted in the colours of 'MT928' as flown by Sqn Ldr G R S McKay with 145 Squadron, the first unit to fly the Mk.VIII operationally.
JOHN M DIBBS – PLANE PICTURE COMPANY

YOUR HIG

His Highness Pratap Singh Gaekwad became the Maharaja of Baroda in the Indian state of Gujarat in 1939. To help the war effort, the peoples of the British Empire were encouraged to donate funds and 'adopt' an RAF squadron and this was reflected in the unit's official title. Following a generous donation of £50,000 by the Maharajah in July 1941, the recently formed 124 Squadron was named as the 'Baroda Squadron'.

Based at Castletown in northern Scotland, the Spitfire-equipped 124 Squadron was commanded by Sqn Ldr Myles Duke-Woolley. Periodically he and is successors wrote to their benefactor to keep him appraised of the exploits of 'his' squadron.

By May 1945 the Baroda Squadron was flying Spitfire IXs from Hutton Cranswick in Yorkshire. On the 15th, CO Sqn Ldr G W Scott sent his final wartime report to the Maharaja of Baroda and it forms the basis of this feature.

ADOPTED BY THE INDIAN STATE OF BARODA, 124 SQUADRON
REGULARLY UPDATED THE MAHARAJA ON THE EXPLOITS OF 'HIS' UNIT, AS
ANDREW THOMAS RECOUNTS

─HNESS...

DRAMATIC RELIEF

"Your Highness, with the end of the war in Europe we are likely to see a number of far-reaching changes concerning the future of the Baroda Squadron. I take this opportunity of reporting to you on activities while it has been under my command.

When I took over in September of last year, operational activity consisted mainly of escorting heavy bombers engaged in neutralising the German war industries of the Rhine area. This was vitally important work, but the only opposition we experienced from the enemy was from flak as most of his fighters, which might interfere with the bombers, were looked after by the Second Tactical Air Force based on the Continent.

Far left
Flt Lt Peter Ayerst was awarded the DFC when he left the 124 Squadron in early 1945.
WG CDR P V AYERST

Left
From March 1943 to July 1944 the Baroda Squadron operated Spitfire VIIs, including EN509.
VIA C H THOMAS

Below left
On Christmas Day 1944 Baroda Squadron pilots met Me 262 jets but they proved too fast to engage.
VIA JOHN WEAL

"THE MOST INTERESTING DIVERSION OCCURRED ON CHRISTMAS DAY WHEN WE MET ONE OR TWO MESSERSCHMITT ME 262S, THE NEW GERMAN JET-PROPELLED FIGHTERS, BUT THESE WERE TOO FAST FOR US AND GOT AWAY."

The result was that there were no combats and we never fired our guns except on the very rare occasions when, by nature of dramatic relief, we were allowed to carry out an independent fighter sweep or armed recce into Germany. The most interesting diversion of this nature occurred on Christmas Day when we met one or two Messerschmitt Me 262s, the new German jet-propelled fighters, but these were too fast for us and got away. By way of compensation, we destroyed four locomotives which we discovered near Coblenz.

Our bomber escorts continued until January and although we encountered quite a lot of flak in varying degrees of accuracy we had no casualties. One isolated incident is worth recording, however. This happened to Flt Lt B R Murphy, our adjutant, who was shot down over Cologne on December 28 [in PL218 while escorting Lancasters to Cologne Author].

His machine eventually caught fire and broke up, but not before he managed to glide sufficiently near our own lines to make good his escape. It was a near thing as Flt Lt Murphy was still entangled in his machine when the wings came off. His parachute operated successfully and he was picked up by the American army and taken to hospital at Aachen. Flt Lt Murphy has now fully recovered and is back with us again."

FIGHTING V-2s

"The New Year brought us some very bad flying weather, but also a refreshing change. Towards the end of 1944 the enemy had started launching V-2s – Hitler's new rocket weapon, against London. This activity became stepped up in January and fresh fighter-bomber squadrons were called upon to reinforce those already in action against the firing sites.

We were one of two squadrons selected for this reinforcement and on January 23 we became non-operational for the purpose of fitting bomb racks to our Spitfires and ➡

124 (BARODA) SQUADRON

Briefly operational during World War One from March to August 1918, serving as a day bomber unit, 124 Squadron was revived on May 10, 1941 at Castletown.

With its links to Baroda, the unit adopted the mongoose for its badge and 'Danger is Our Opportunity' as its motto. Renowned for its agility and ferocity in killing, the mongoose was an appropriate emblem for a fighter squadron with Indian links.

Above
Bomber escorts to towns in the Ruhr occupied 124 Squadron during September 1944.
GP CAPT H W HARRISON

Right
The main threat during bomber escorts was flak, particularly from the deadly 88mm gun.
VIA JOHN WEAL

undergoing intensive training for dive-bombing. Weather was unsatisfactory for practice but we persevered at every available opportunity and on February 5 we were able to report ourselves fully ready to go into action.

On February 10 we took off from Manston for the last time to move to our new headquarters at Coltishall near Norwich. The move did us all a lot of good. In the first place, we were kept extremely busy, as weather did not interfere with our work to anything like the same extent that it did on bomber escorts.

In the second place, from the point of view of comfort, Coltishall was a great advance on Manston. Our new station had suffered not at all by enemy action, and we operated under an almost peacetime

"WE HAD HOPED THAT BEFORE THE END WE MIGHT HAVE HAD THE OPPORTUNITY OF SEEING THE REICH CAPITAL FROM THE AIR, BUT THE SWIFTNESS OF THE ENEMY COLLAPSE DENIED US THAT PRIVILEGE..."

establishment. The comfortable quarters for our groundcrews were particularly welcome after the damp wooden huts of Manston, and the resulting stimulus to morale was very noticeable.

We finally went into action on the 14th and from this date onwards we were kept fully occupied. The new work, which consisted in dive-bombing storage sites for the 'V-weapon', strafing transport and breaking up railways lines, was, we found, very interesting and particularly satisfying.

We could see the results of our efforts much more directly than at any time since we started bomber escort work and the squadron quickly settled down to obtain very good results. It was particularly satisfactory to see the effect of our efforts reflected in the V-2 activity against London.

Our success was not accomplished without some casualties, however, and during the period of dive-bombing activity we lost four pilots, all of them comparative newcomers, but still a tragic loss to the squadron. [Including F/Sgt P B Allen who died on February 15; Flt Lt C J Maltby on March 25 and F/Sgt C M Lett on March 30.]"

BREAKTHROUGH

"With the breakthrough into northern Holland at the end of March by the 21st Army Group, enemy rocket activity came to an end and we left Coltishall to resume our bomber escort work; this time operating from Hawkinge. This was a very good station but as far as operations went it was really only a servicing base as the actual escorts were conducted from airfields

in Holland and Belgium, taken over from the Second Tactical Air Force which had moved forward to keep pace with the retreating and disorganised German armies.

Bomber escorts from Hawkinge were without incident, but they showed us a lot of new enemy territory. Of these missions, the most spectacular to watch was that involving the bombing of the island fortress of Heligoland on April 18.

We had hoped that before the end we might have had the opportunity of seeing the Reich capital from the air, but the swiftness of the enemy collapse denied us that privilege, and before the end of April our escort work came to a standstill.

Our last operational work before the final stand-down was to remain at readiness, to counter any last throw by the enemy from air

Above
Led by Spitfire IX PV303, the Baroda Squadron flew an immaculate flypast for the Maharaja's visit on April 20, 1945.
GP CAPT H W HARRISON

bases in Norway. This was done from our present station, Hutton Cranswick in Yorkshire, and now that the surrender has come we look forward to fresh developments."

HIGH STANDARDS

"As regards social and personal news, you will have heard through Sir Frank Brown of the squadron's magnificent activities at the end of the last year through your great generosity. [Sir Frank was the Secretary of the East Indies Association.]

The all-ranks party and dance at Westcliff Theatre and the reception at the Savoy were considered the leading social events in the life of the squadron so far. With the advent of Christmas, we inaugurated a series of unit and echelon parties

at Manston, where we possessed accommodation particularly suited for functions of this kind. These social events did much to sustain morale and good relations between pilots and groundcrews reached a new high level.

At the end of January our late CO and Wing Leader, Wg Cdr T Balmforth DFC, retired from operations to go on a staff college course under the US Army in America. We were all sorry to see him go, but he had earned a well-deserved rest and it was particularly gratifying to learn later that he had been awarded the DSO for his work in Fighter Command.

Another decoration which came to the squadron was to Flt Lt P V Ayerst who was awarded the DFC. He had completed a long and

distinguished tour of operations since the Battle of France in 1940. At the end of January, he left to become a test pilot.

Another pilot to leave us at the beginning of the year was Flt Lt M O Wilson who was earmarked for instructional work at an Operational Training Unit. On leaving us he did a course at Central Gunnery School, where he distinguished himself by obtaining the highest category of pass awarded.

Further credit to the squadron

Above
A NAAFI van in front of Meteor IIIs of 124 Squadron.
GP CAPT H W HARRISON

> "ON JUNE 20 HARRISON WELCOMED HIS HIGHNESS THE MAHARAJA OF BARODA WHO HAD COME TO HUTTON CRANSWICK TO VISIT 'HIS' SQUADRON. HE INSPECTED THE LINE-UP OF SPITFIRES, EACH DECORATED WITH THE UNIT BADGE – A MONGOOSE – BEFORE AN IMMACULATE FLYPAST WAS STAGED IN SALUTE OF THE DISTINGUISHED GUEST."

Left
On April 20, 1945 the Maharaja of Baroda visited and inspected 'his' squadron at Hutton Cranswick. His Highness (centre) is accompanied by Station CO Wg Cdr Saunders (right) and Sqn Ldr Jerry Harrison OC 124 Sqn (left). Note the mongoose on the cowling of the Spitfire on the right. GP CAPT H W HARRISON

Far left
In early 1945 the Baroda Squadron switched to fighter-bomber attacks on V-2 rocket sites in Holland. VIA JOHN WEAL

was achieved by Flt Lt C K Grey, the commander of 'A' Flight, who completed a very successful course at the Royal Navy School of Air Warfare. The results he obtained there were the highest in the history of the school, which reflects the high standard of flying existing in this squadron.

As a result of the operational work completed these past eight months, we shall shortly be losing most of the experienced pilots who have made this squadron the efficient

fighting unit it has been during their stay. They will, however, be taking over important instructional and experimental work so vital to the future development of the RAF.

We shall be seeing a lot of new faces in the immediate future, but the few old pilots who remain have the traditions of the Baroda Squadron behind them and they will guide the newcomers in the way they have to go.

Past members of 124 Squadron continue to keep in touch with us and we have frequent visits from them. All send their greetings to you and the unit thanks you again for all you have done to make life in the Baroda Squadron so happy."
Sqn Ldr G W Scott,
CO 124 (Baroda) Squadron

EPILOGUE
A couple of weeks after writing this letter Sqn Ldr Scott was replaced as CO by Sqn Ldr H W 'Jerry' Harrison. On June 20 Harrison welcomed His Highness the Maharaja of Baroda who had come to Hutton Cranswick to visit 'his'

squadron. He inspected the line-up of Spitfires, each decorated with the unit badge – a mongoose – before an immaculate flypast was staged in salute of the distinguished guest.

In his letter, Sqn Ldr Scott had hinted at changes and these occurred on August 21 when the first Gloster Meteor III jets arrived to begin re-equipment. The pilots soon converted and Jerry Harrison was later able to report to His Highness: "Following our conversion we moved to Bentwaters on October 5. Our activities were the normal squadron training exercises and we spent a lot of time doing rehearsals for the Victory Flypast."

Despite having the honour of being one of the RAF's first jet squadrons, as peacetime cuts took effect there was a desire to keep longer-serving units in being. Thus 124 Squadron disbanded on April 1, 1946 and was immediately re-formed as 56 Squadron, itself a very distinguished fighter unit. However, the Baroda Squadron had gone out on jet wings and with real style. ●

THE ULTIMATE
DAY FIGHT

Piloting a Spitfire V out of Hornchurch on June 2, 1942 Flt Lt John Kingaby got the better of a Focke-Wulf Fw 190 and was granted a 'damaged' towards his already impressive tally of combat victories. The following month, Flt Lt Kingaby's unit, 64 Squadron, started conversion to Mk.IXs and quickly the new variant was to prove its worth.

Off Boulogne on July 30, this time at the helm of Mk.IX BR600, Flt Lt Kingaby took on another Fw 190 and he was credited with a 'kill'. It was his first and the first for the Mk.IX. Flt Lt Kingaby went on to add three Fw 190s to his victories – reaching 21 plus two 'shared'.

Leap-frogging the more refined Mk.VIII into service, the Mk.IX was a pragmatic upgrade of the combat-proven Mk.V, fitted with a supercharged Merlin 61 to help bridge the gap when encountering the Fw 190. With more than 5,000 built, the Mk.IX was the second most produced Spitfire. The final examples were completed in the summer of 1945.

It was 1947 when the RAF

SPITFIRE IX FACTFILE

With under-fuselage slipper tank and painted in 'Invasion' stripes, Mk.IX MJ329 used its bomb racks to great effect with the so-called 'Modification XXX' – carrying much-needed kegs of beer to the D-Day beachhead. It was serving with 412 Squadron RCAF at this time. KEY-GORDON SWANBOROUGH COLLECTION

Engine:	Rolls-Royce Merlin 61, 63, 65A, or 66 – HF.IX Merlin 66 rated at 1,475hp (1,100kW)
Statistics:	Dimensions: (HF.IX) Span 36ft 10in (11.23m) Length 31ft 4in (9.55m) Height 11ft 5in (3.48m) Weights: Empty 5,800lb (2,631kg) Loaded 7,296lb (3,309kg) Performance: Max speed 408mph (657km/h) Service ceiling 43,000ft (13,106m)
Armament:	Wing armament variations: eight 0.303in machine guns; four 0.303in machine guns and two 20mm cannons; four 20mm cannon and two 0.303in machine guns. Up to a 1,000lb (454kg) bomb under the centre section
First flown:	September 20, 1941 from Hucknall, Mk.III N3297 serving as the development prototype
Number built:	5,440 by Supermarine and Castle Bromwich
Sub-Variants:	F, LF and HF versions. Conversions to tac-recce FR.IX and to photo-recce PR.IX, Floatplane – see Sea Boots, Tr.9 two-seater – see overleaf, plus in-field two-seat UTI trainers in USSR

ER?

retired its last frontline Mk.IXs. The type was widely exported and it formed the basis of the definitive two-seat version — see overleaf.

Below
A couple of Spitfires are so well-known and regarded that they are referred to by just their serial numbers. Probably the most famous of this elite is Mk.IX MH434 (G-ASJV) of the Old Flying Machine Company. In the confines of a caption, its illustrious heritage can only be hinted at. Test flown at Castle Bromwich by Alex Henshaw in August 1943, it was issued to 222 (Natal) Squadron at Hornchurch that month, becoming 'ZD-B'. It was flown by South African Flt Lt Henry Lardner-Burke and on August 27 he shot down an Fw 190 and damaged another. He went on to destroy a further '190 on September 5, also in MH434. In 1947 the Mk.IX was transferred to the Royal Netherlands Air Force and it saw action in Java. It next served with the Belgian Air Force as an advanced trainer from 1953 until 1956. Then it began a life as a civilian that is also the stuff of legend, but for another time. Today MH434 is cherished at Duxford, proudly flying in Flt Lt Lardner-Burke's markings. JOHN M DIBBS - PLANE PICTURE COMPANY

Left
Battle of Britain Memorial Flight Mk.IX MK356 wore the winged sword badge and markings of 601 (County of London) Squadron for the 2008 to 2013 seasons. This represented MJ250, flown by 601's Flt Lt Desmond Ibbotson in Italy, 1944.
JOHN M DIBBS - PLANE PICTURE COMPANY

A SPITFIRE
MADE FOR

During World War Two there were a few examples of 'in-field' two-seat conversions of Spitfires, but a dedicated trainer was not required. This changed in the immediate post-war period, when it became clear that the Spitfire, and to a lesser extent the Seafire, had export potential and that a market existed for a two-seater.

Despite a large stock of Mk.IXs being available, Vickers opted for 1944-built Mk.VIII MT818 in early 1946 and it was moved to Chilbolton for conversion to Tr.VIII status. Considerable re-engineering was involved, moving the cockpit *forward* so the instructor's 'office' could be installed and above and behind. To achieve this, the forward fuel tank was decreased in size and wing tanks introduced to keep the endurance up to the levels that

meaningful training sessions would require.

With the 'B Condition' (or 'trade-plate') markings N32, the two-seater prototype made its first flight on September 9, 1946. Vickers undertook an arduous campaign to get the RAF to adopt a Spitfire fighter-trainer, but the force preferred to stick with the North American Harvard. Prototype MT818 survives; it is nearing the

South African-born Jackie Sorour flew as a ferry pilot for the Air Transport Auxiliary during World War Two. On April 29, 1944 she strapped into Spitfire IX ML407 at 33 Maintenance Unit, Lyneham, and flew it to the advanced airstrip at Selsey in Sussex. There she handed it over to 485 Squadron RNZAF and the following day the Spitfire was tested by New Zealander Fg Off 'Johnnie' Houlton. In the early 1990s, Jackie Moggridge (nee Sorour), Johnnie Houlton and ML407 had a reunion at Duxford.

TWO

end of a restoration at Booker.
Vickers sold 20 Tr.IX conversions to existing Spitfire operators: Egypt, India, Ireland and the Netherlands. The Irish Air Corps took delivery of six two-seaters in 1951, retiring the last examples in August 1961 and all but one survives. The allure of a two-seater Spitfire and the recent Civil Aviation Authority decision to grant certain operators the ability to take members of the public flying

has meant several single-seater restorations have been completed as Tr.IXs with others in the pipeline.

Below

Spitfire Tr.IX ML407 (G-LFIX) is another that is widely known by just its serial number, but it also delights in another name: 'The Grace Spitfire'. Delivered to the Irish Air Corps on July 30, 1951, it was acquired by the late Nick Grace and restored, first flying as a 'warbird' on April 16, 1985. Nick's more streamlined, fighter-like canopy has been adopted by other two-seater conversions. Today, ML407 is flown by Carolyn Grace and her son, Richard. On D-Day, June 6, 1944, ML407 was with 485 Squadron RNZAF and it was being flown by 'Kiwi' Fg Off 'Johnnie' Houlton, he engaged a Junkers Ju 88 and shot it down – the first enemy aircraft to fall that day. Today, ML407 wears the same markings and codes it wore on that historic day. BOTH JOHN M DIBBS – PLANE PICTURE COMPANY

BY THE THOUSAND

JONATHAN GARRAWAY EXAMINES THE VAST CASTLE BROMWICH SPITFIRE FACTORY AND ITS PRODIGIOUS OUTPUT

Euphoria and relief are common emotions experienced whenever a prototype takes to the air for the first time. Crucial though that event might be, by far the biggest hurdle is getting the new design into production. Just 90 days after 'Mutt' Summers carried out the maiden flight of Supermarine Type 300 K5054 (see page 6) on June 3, 1936 the Air Ministry placed an order for 310 fully militarised versions ready for frontline service.

Champagne corks may have been popping but, despite being part of the giant conglomerate Vickers-Armstrongs, Supermarine was a small concern that was finding building Walrus amphibians challenging. Mass manufacturing a state-of-the-art fighter was a daunting prospect.

Problems emerged at an alarming rate. A string of sub-contractors was engaged to help with the massive capacity expansion required. Co-ordinating ten different companies, all reliant on one another to keep the flow going, was a never-ending ordeal. (This was not a new problem and it still rears its head, as Airbus and Boeing can testify.)

That beautiful elliptical wing was a nightmare to build and a specification change to the leading edge did not help the timetable. Production of fuselages was out-pacing the wings and Supermarine was taking a lot of the flak from the Air Ministry. Alternatives needed to be considered: perhaps the Itchen and Woolston factories in Southampton were better suited to other, less complex, types?

The prospect that Supermarine could switch to building the 'rival' Hurricane was real, but other options took priority. The Air Ministry pondered letting Supermarine take over Lysander production from Yeovil-based Westland and perhaps the same company's twin-engined Whirlwind fighter. Another twin considered was the Bristol Beaufighter. Westland had started making wing ribs for Supermarine in 1936 and from 1939 took on manufacturing entire Spitfires.

SHADOW FACTORY
As Supermarine fought to overcome a very steep learning curve, the Air Ministry realised that removing tooling from the Southampton plants would hinder output of Spitfires and a more radical solution was needed. A second contract for 200 Spitfire Is was placed with Woolston in March 1938.

Talks began in May with a giant of the manufacturing process, motor vehicle mogul William Morris – Lord Nuffield. The idea of 'Shadow Factories' – well-proven industries building aircraft to supplement the original constructor – had been well established in World War One. The mass production skills of the Nuffield Organisation could transform Spitfire output. Morris talked of an initial batch of 1,000.

Also in May 1938, the first production Spitfire, Mk.I K9787, first took to the skies at Eastleigh, 27 months after the prototype. In August, 19 Squadron at Duxford became

"THAT BEAUTIFUL ELLIPTICAL WING WAS A NIGHTMARE TO BUILD AND A SPECIFICATION CHANGE TO THE LEADING EDGE DID NOT HELP THE TIMETABLE. PRODUCTION OF FUSELAGES WAS OUT-PACING THE WINGS..."

operational and reached full strength – 16 aircraft – when K9811 was delivered on November 11. By that time just over 200 Hurricanes were in squadron service.

Nuffield began planning a huge factory with the capability to churn out a maximum of 60 Spitfires a week. Meanwhile there was much debate regarding where it could be built. Liverpool, far away from enemy bombers and with a ready workforce, was prominent. Nuffield held out for the area he knew well, the Midlands.

Land held by Birmingham Corporation and tyre manufacturer Dunlop adjacent to Castle Bromwich airfield, to the east of Birmingham was ideal and all 1,414 acres was acquired at £1,000 per acre. A huge building, used for the assembly of Handley O/400 bombers in 1918 and the venue for the February 1937 British Industries Fair, was close by and was taken over. Construction of the vast factory – the Castle Bromwich Aircraft Factory (CBAF) began on July 12, 1938. Including all machinery, the entire plant cost £4 million.

Nuffield pulled out of the whole deal in the spring of 1940. He had clashed

Left
The flight line at Castle Bromwich in 1944 with massed Spitfire IXs and two Lancasters.

Below
Running through the main site was 'Central Avenue', which was bridged at several points by walkways from one hall to another.

CAUSE AND EFFECT

Birmingham-Minworth
Flugzeugzellenwerk (Montagehalle)

Birmingham was blitzed by the Luftwaffe several times from 1940 through to 1943, with horrific loss of life and property. The Castle Bromwich Aircraft Factory (CBAF) was on the receiving end on the night of August 13/14, 1940, just a fraction of the damage is illustrated below. Seven people perished in the raid and another 41 were badly injured, but production was hardly interrupted.

A Luftwaffe target chart (above), dated September 3, 1940 was probably taken for post-raid damage assessment and it was updated in September 1942. Clear on the chart is the railway line running from the northwest, with one section taking a sharp curve to the east, in the direction of central Birmingham. This acted as the eastern and southern boundary of the airfield and factory site. Wending its way across the middle of the target, and forming the northern boundary, is the Birmingham and Fazeley Canal. On the extreme lower left is part of the huge CBAF site and to the right of that the British Industries Fair building.

In the centre is the all-grass runway – 'Rollbahn' – complete with 'hedges' painted on the airfield as camouflage. Opposite is the square flight shed which the Luftwaffe labelled as a 'Montagehalle' (assembly hall) surrounded by a 'Lagerplatze' (stockyard, perhaps more appropriately flight line or 'ramp').

with Max Aitken, Lord Beaverbrook, the newspaper magnate nominated to run the Ministry of Aircraft Production. Establishing a factory of such spectacular size, setting up the machinery and getting the assembly lines rolling was a huge achievement, so Nuffield had not left his country in the lurch. His Morris Motors started to build Tiger Moths at Cowley in 1940, allowing de Havilland to concentrate on the incredible Mosquito at Hatfield.

Filling the void, staff from Vickers-Armstrongs took on the management of CBAF in May 1940. The first 'Castle Brom' Spitfire, Mk.II P7280, was delivered to Boscombe Down on June 27, 1940. It was the first of thousands.

A SHEER DREAM

Synonymous with CBAF was its chief test pilot, Alex Henshaw, who had become a legend for his air racing prowess and long-distance flights. His greatest pre-war exploit was a record-breaking out-and-back flight to the Cape of Good Hope, South Africa in the diminutive single-seat Percival ➡

Clockwise from left
The main factory site from a DH Dominie; looking south towards the town of Castle Bromwich. Today the M6 motorway runs across the very top of the picture with central Birmingham off to the right.

Tropical filter-fitted Spitfire V ER810 at Castle Bromwich in October 1942. It carries the name 'Inca' on the forward fuselage, funded by the people of Lima, Peru.

Castle Bromwich test pilots, left to right: Flt Lt J Rosser, Alex Henshaw, Norwegian Captain Olav Ullstad and Czechoslovakian Flt Lt Venda Jicha.

The flight sheds, looking east.

"THE MASS PRODUCTION SKILLS OF THE NUFFIELD ORGANISATION COULD TRANSFORM SPITFIRE OUTPUT. MORRIS TALKED OF AN INITIAL BATCH OF 1,000."

Above
The pattern makers' shop; working on items for Lancasters as well as Spitfires.

Above right
Part of the dope room; sewing fabric on Spitfire rudders.

Below
The vast production jig and tool drawing office.

Mew Gull G-AEXF in February 1939.

Alex volunteered for the RAF in 1939, aged 27. While he was waiting for a reply, Vickers approached him to become a test pilot at Brooklands, checking out Wellingtons. Then he met Supermarine chief test pilot Jeffrey Quill who saw in Alex the perfect personality for the Spitfire. Jeffrey had him moved to Eastleigh and there Alex sampled the first of 2,300-plus Spitfires he was to fly. In his exceptional book *Sigh for a Merlin*, the love Alex developed for the fighter leaps out of every page, for him "it was a sheer dream".

On June 1, 1940 Alex took on the flight test department at 'Castle Brom' and established a gifted team around him. Alex flew most of the 305 Lancasters that were also built at CBAF. At least once, Alex barrel-rolled a 'Lanc' and he described the bomber as finely tuned and exceptionally reliable.

There are many stories of Alex's time at CBAF – but just two more will have to suffice. To launch Birmingham's Spitfire Fund, the Lord Mayor invited him to carry out a flypast alongside the town hall in front of gathered honoured guests and the public. It was September 18, 1940 and Alex made an unforgettable 'entrance' in Spitfire II P7426. Flying *inverted* at high speed, the fighter was below roof height! The mayor was not best pleased. To quote Alex's logbook: "Instructed to demonstrate over Birmingham. Chaos ensued!"

Testing Spitfire IX MJ190 on October 13, 1943 the engine broke up while Alex was flying at 470mph (756km/h). The entry in his fifth logbook makes a terrifying experience seem almost run-of-the-mill: "Flung out of machine with badly torn parachute. Three complete panels missing and canopy held together by slender pieces of thread for 15,000ft."

45 A WEEK

Statistics for output at CBAF vary and are hotly disputed in some quarters. Turning to the last page of Henshaw's *Sigh for a Merlin*, the great man sums up CBAF Spitfires as follows: 11,694 Spitfires built (including the dispersal factories at Cosford and Desford that CBAF oversaw), requiring 33,918 test flights to sign them off ready for collection by the RAF.

"FLYING INVERTED AT HIGH SPEED, THE FIGHTER WAS BELOW ROOF HEIGHT! THE MAYOR WAS NOT BEST PLEASED. TO QUOTE ALEX'S LOGBOOK: 'INSTRUCTED TO DEMONSTRATE OVER BIRMINGHAM. CHAOS ENSUED!'"

The last complete Spitfire flown from Castle Bromwich was Mk.22 PK614 on November 30, 1945. It was issued to the RAF in January 1946. Since Mk.II P7280 emerged in June 1940 that makes an average of just shy of 45 Spitfires a week.

Fuselages and sub-assemblies continued to be put together as production tapered out. The last fuselage down the track was Mk.22 PK726, which was destined to be completed as an Mk.24 at South Marston in March 1946. This machine was bedecked with comments and poems by the CBAF workforce, one of which was full of hope that another type would be built on the site:

"This is the last, this is the end. After many an ache, many a bend. We pass it to you without any tears. For we may 'Meteor' yet in future years." ●

PHOTO-RECCE
WORKHC

With its stable flight characteristics, high speed and high-altitude performance, the Spitfire was a natural choice for use in the photo-reconnaissance (PR) role. Initially, this involved conversions of Mk.Is and some Mk.IX, but later small numbers of the purpose-developed PR.X and the pressurised PR.XIII appeared.

The first dedicated PR version was the Mk.XI, based upon the Mk.IX airframe. The first example, BS497, started trials in November 1942. The PR.XI could carry a pair of palletised F24 cameras, one in each wing. In the rear fuselage three larger-lends F24s could be carried in

SPITFIRE XI FACTFILE

Engine:	Rolls-Royce Merlin 61, 63 or 70 – Merlin 70 rated at 1,475hp (1,100kW)
Statistics:	Dimensions: Span 36ft 10in (11.23m) Length 30ft 4¹/₂in (9.25m) Weights: Empty 5,575lb (2,529kg) Loaded 7,872lb (3,571kg) Performance: Max speed 417mph (671km/h) Service ceiling 44,000ft (13,411m)
Armament:	None
First flown	January 1943, EN341, first production example, issued to service
Number built:	464 by Supermarine

Built in late 1943, PR.XI PA846 was shipped to India in January 1944. There it joined 681 Squadron, moving to Mingaladon, Burma, from May 1945. The PR.XIs of 681 provided vital photo-recce of Japanese troop and ship movements. KEY-GORDON SWANBOROUGH COLLECTION

RSE

combinations of vertical and oblique fittings.

At the home of British PR flying, Benson in Oxfordshire, the first unit to adopt the PR.XI was 541 Squadron from December 1942. The final examples were retired by this unit as late as October 1946. Production of Mk.XIs came to an end in early 1945.

Below

Peter Teichman's Hangar 11 Collection, based at North Weald, treasures the only flying PR.XI, PL965 (G-MKXI). It wears the colours and markings of its first operational unit, 16 Squadron. Operating from Northolt from January 1944, it later flew from airfields in France and the Netherlands, until September. It was delivered to the Royal Netherlands Air Force in July 1947 for use as an instructional airframe before moving to the museum at Overloon in 1960. Brought to the UK in 1987, it was returned to airworthy condition and had its first post-restoration flight in December 1992 from Rochester. After a brief period in the USA, PL965 was acquired by Peter Teichman in 2004 and has been a regular on the UK airshow 'circuit' since.

JOHN M DIBBS – PLANE PICTURE COMPANY

UNDER
MANY FLAGS

FROM ARGENTINA TO YUGOSLAVIA, AND MANY
COUNTRIES IN BETWEEN, SPITFIRES AND SEAFIRES
WERE WIDELY EXPORTED – WITNESS
THIS SELECTION

Top
Israel gathered a variety of warplanes for its war on independence in 1948-1949,
receiving Spitfires mostly from former Czechoslovakian stocks. The type was finally
retired in 1956. Wearing the red and white tail colours of 105 Squadron Mk.IX '17'
(full serial 2017) was ferried to Israel from Prague in December 1948. It served until
being written off in a flying accident in December 1954.

Above
A batch of 20 Seafire XVs, stripped of naval gear, was ordered by the newly-
established Union of Burma Air Force in 1951. They were flight tested in the UK
wearing 'B' Condition – or 'trade-plate' – markings before being shipped to Burma
(now Myanmar) in 1952. Last serving with 780 Squadron Mk.XV SR642 was test flown
as G-15-214; it served in Burma as UB403 until the mid-1950s.

Right
Today, Spitfires are in private ownership worldwide; but in the immediate post-war
period this was unheard of. James and Jack Storey acquired Spitfire PR.XI PL972
from Vickers in April 1947: it came complete with three F24 cameras, wing fuel tanks
and a 'slipper' tank under the centre section. The pair planned to use the Spitfire
for a survey contract in Argentina and it was registered as LV-NMZ accordingly. It
arrived in Buenos Aires in May 1947, but nothing came of the contract and LV-NMZ
was taken over by the air force. The aircraft had been scrapped by the mid-1950s.

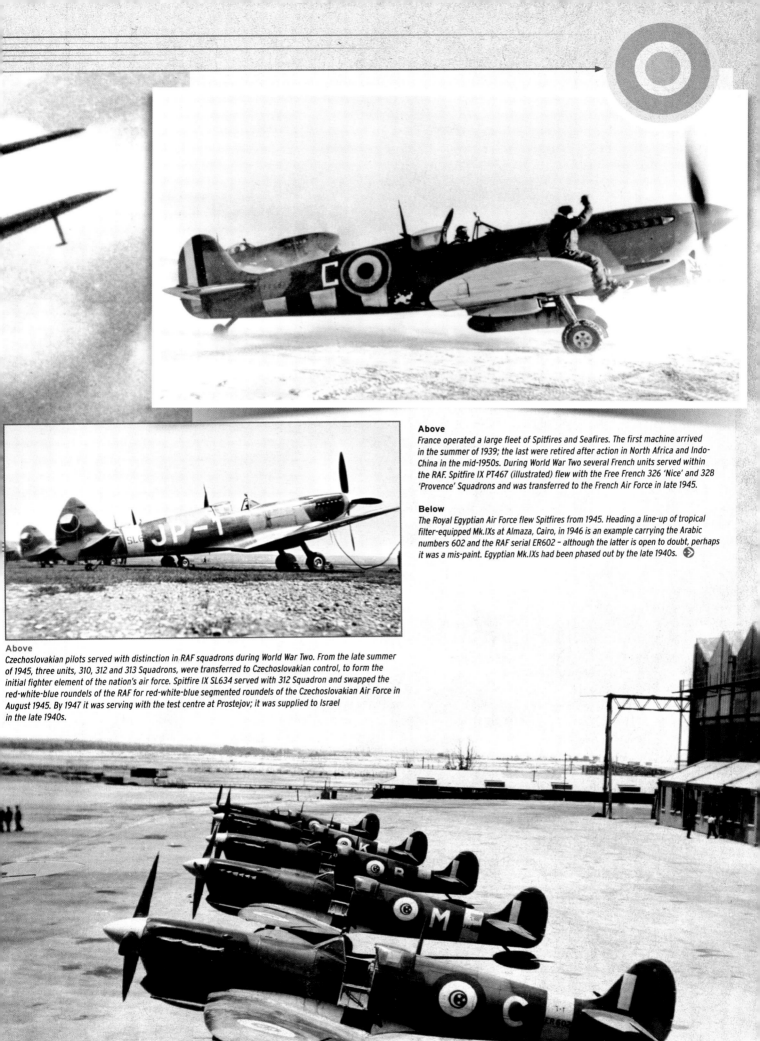

Above

France operated a large fleet of Spitfires and Seafires. The first machine arrived in the summer of 1939; the last were retired after action in North Africa and Indo-China in the mid-1950s. During World War Two several French units served within the RAF. Spitfire IX PT467 (illustrated) flew with the Free French 326 'Nice' and 328 'Provence' Squadrons and was transferred to the French Air Force in late 1945.

Below

The Royal Egyptian Air Force flew Spitfires from 1945. Heading a line-up of tropical filter-equipped Mk.IXs at Almaza, Cairo, in 1946 is an example carrying the Arabic numbers 602 and the RAF serial ER602 – although the latter is open to doubt, perhaps it was a mis-paint. Egyptian Mk.IXs had been phased out by the late 1940s. ➡

Above

Czechoslovakian pilots served with distinction in RAF squadrons during World War Two. From the late summer of 1945, three units, 310, 312 and 313 Squadrons, were transferred to Czechoslovakian control, to form the initial fighter element of the nation's air force. Spitfire IX SL634 served with 312 Squadron and swapped the red-white-blue roundels of the RAF for red-white-blue segmented roundels of the Czechoslovakian Air Force in August 1945. By 1947 it was serving with the test centre at Prostejov; it was supplied to Israel in the late 1940s.

On September 21, 1939 Spitfire I L1090 was unveiled at the US Army Air Corps flight test and evaluation centre at Patterson Field, Dayton, Ohio – the first time the new type had been seen in the USA. After the Americans had tried it out, it was flown at Uplands, Ottawa, in May 1940 for assessment by the RCAF.

Turkey was an early Spitfire customer; taking delivery of a trio of Mk.Is in September 1939. From 1944 Mk.Vs were delivered, with Mk.IXs (illustrated) and PR.XIXs following in 1949. Operational flying is believed to have ceased in the first years of the 1950s.

Above
The Netherlands was hoping to acquire Spitfires as early as 1939, but it was not to be. Two Dutch squadrons within the RAF flew Spitfires during the war. Post-war, a fleet of predominantly Mk.IXs was operated, some flying combat missions in the Dutch East Indies – Java. Spitfire IXs H-30 and H-31 were allocated from RAF stocks (serials MJ828 and MJ152 respectively) and delivered to Amsterdam in June 1947. Of this pair, H-30 was the longest lived, being withdrawn from use in 1954.

Right
Designated S 31 by the Swedish Air Force, 50 Spitfire PR.XIXs served with F11 Wing on long-range sorties between 1948 and 1955. High-flying Swedish PR.XIXs were used for flights across the Baltic Sea and for perilous missions beyond the Arctic Circle towards the Soviet naval bases in the Murmansk area.

Above
Yugoslav personnel served with 352 Squadron which formed up in Italy in the spring of 1944, replacing its Hurricanes for Spitfire Vs in June. By June 1945 the unit was at Pykos in Yugoslavia, its aircraft wearing red stars over the RAF roundels in celebration of the return to the homeland. The squadron's Mk.Vs (including JK544, illustrated) were returned to RAF control and from 1946 a mixture of Mk.Vs and Mk.IXs were delivered. These served until 1952.

Below
American use of Spitfires in the European theatre was extensive, starting with the famed 'Eagle' squadrons – 71, 121, 133 that were later absorbed into the USAAF as, respectively, the 334th, 335th and 336th Fighter Squadrons of the 4th Fighter Group. Spitfire V BL680 served with the 7th Photographic Reconnaissance Group at Mount Farm in 1944. ALL KEY COLLECTION ●

GRIFFON
TO THE FORE

Phenomenal though it was, the Rolls-Royce Merlin could be developed only so far. When the Spitfire entered operational service in 1938, the Merlin II was rated at 900hp and by 1941 the Merlin 66 fitted to Spitfire IXs was generating 1,475hp. Working from a starting output of 1,500hp the Griffon was developed as a scaled-up Merlin, necessitating a much redesigned and longer Spitfire.

The first variant to take the Griffon was a pair of developmental Mk.IVs from November 1941 – these were redesignated Mk.XX in March 1942. A run of 100 Mk.XIIs began the following month, becoming adept at intercepting 'tip-and-run'

SPITFIRE XIV FACTFILE

First flown at Aldermaston by test pilot Mike Lithgow on February 2, 1945 fighter-recce configured 'low-back' Mk.XIV MV363 was shipped to India and served with 11 Squadron gaining the name 'Mary' on its cowling. The unit flew Mk.XIVs from the summer of 1945 to early 1948, from India, Malaya and finally with the occupation forces in Japan. KEY COLLECTION

Engine:	Rolls-Royce Griffon 65 of 2,025hp (1,529kW)
Statistics:	Dimensions: Span 36ft 10in (11.23m) Length 32ft 8in (9.96m) Height 11ft 8in (3.55m) Weights: Empty 6,376lb (2,892kg) Loaded 8,475lb (3,844kg) Performance: Max speed 439mph (707km/h) Service ceiling 43,000ft (13,106m)
Armament:	F or FR.XIVc, four 0.303in machine guns and two 20mm cannons; F or FR.XIVe, two 0.303in machine guns and two 20mm cannons. Single 250lb (113kg) or 500lb (227kg) bomb under the centre section
First flown:	September 7, 1943, converted Mk.VIII JF317 acting as series prototype. First production Mk.XIV, RB140, issued to service December 20, 1943
Number built:	957 by Supermarine

Fw 190 fighter-bombers.

The Mk.XIV, available in both 'high-back' and bubble canopy-equipped 'low-back' options, had enlarged tail surfaces and a longer fuselage, it featured a five-bladed propeller to absorb an impressive 2,050hp from its Griffon 65. Entering service with 610 (County of Chester) Squadron in January 1944, Spitfire XIVs went on to acquit themselves well in campaigns against V-1 'Doodlebugs'. Production was complete by the summer of 1945.

The Merlin still had plenty of potential in it and it remained in production post-war. Far from replacing its forebear, the Griffon added to the piston power Rolls-Royce had to offer.

Below
Built in the spring of 1945, Mk.XIV SM832 went on to enjoy a long and cosmopolitan life. Shipped to India it saw no RAF service and by 1947 was in use by the Indian Air Force as an instructional airframe. Brought to the UK in 1978, it was restored and flew again (as G-WWII) in May 1995, wearing its present-day RAF South East Asia Command colours and the mailed fist badge of 17 Squadron, operating from Singapore and Malaya in late 1945. Moving to France in 1998, SM832 returned to the UK in 2002 before crossing to the Atlantic to the USA in 2004.
JOHN M DIBBS – PLANE PICTURE COMPANY

BETWEEN A ROCK
AND A H

Above
Spitfire FR.XVIIIs TZ233 (rear) and TP391 of 208 Squadron over the Mediterranean.

Right
Fg Off Roy Bowie entertaining children at Eastleigh, Nairobi.

Having spent the previous 15 months fighting its way up Italy in support of the Allied advance, 208 Squadron had reached Villafranca near Verona by April 1945. Equipped with Spitfire IXs, it had flown with distinction in the fighter-reconnaissance role, a dangerous activity in which ten pilots had been lost.

The squadron was the only one of the 285 Wing to survive the transition to peace. By the end of June 1945 it was heading to Palestine, not for the first time during its 35 years' service in the Middle East.

By the end of July the squadron was settled at Ramat David, near Haifa. Training with the army resumed and daily sorties were flown to check the security of oil pipelines running west from Iraq to Haifa on the Mediterranean coast. A few weeks later 208 moved to the better-equipped airfield at Petah Tiqva near Tel Aviv.

In the following months the political situation deteriorated. After the horrors of the Holocaust, Jewish survivors of Hitler's purges would no longer accept a pre-war agreement to limit the number of Jews settling in Palestine, as their national home, without prejudice to the rights of the existing non-Jewish population. Hard-line Zionists demanded an immediate admission of 100,000 – which was unacceptable to Britain and led to the creation of an extremely well organised movement to bring in immigrants by every available means.

Opposing any major influx of a Jewish population was an Arab nationalist movement which had grown during the war years. It was inevitable that the two factions were on a collision course.

MAXIMUM READINESS
RAF units, including 208 Squadron, were tasked with monitoring illegal ship movements carrying immigrants. In addition, 208 extended its traditional army co-operation role to include exercises with the Palestine Police Force, which was British-led and administered. Flying concentrated on training with local ground units and regular reconnaissance to check the effectiveness of roadblocks and the security of the pipelines.

Rising tension saw RAF units brought to a state of maximum defence readiness on January 17, 1946, with 208 Squadron maintaining two aircraft at 30 minutes' readiness.

A Jewish underground terrorist

ARD PLACE

DURING 1947 AND 1948 THE RAF WAS IN THE MIDDLE OF A POWER STRUGGLE IN PALESTINE. **GRAHAM PITCHFORK** DESCRIBES A SITUATION THAT SAW SPITFIRES FIGHTING SPITFIRES

organisation then began taking reprisals against the RAF for its role in anti-immigrant shipping patrols. After sporadic attacks in January and February, which included immobilising the main radar station at Mount Carmel, a co-ordinated and simultaneous strike targeted three airfields during the night of February 25/26.

At Petah Tiqva, the first intimation of the attack came at 20:40 hours when explosions were heard among the dispersed aircraft. RAF Regiment armoured cars rushed to the scene and came under heavy fire from terrorists outside the perimeter. Explosives placed in radiators or cockpits destroyed seven Spitfires of 32 and 208 Squadrons. The saboteurs escaped and similar attacks against other RAF airfields in Palestine led to the loss of more aircraft.

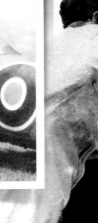

CRISIS POINT

Moving to Ein Shemer – on the Mediterranean coast

20 miles (32km) south of Haifa – in June 1946, 208 Squadron settled into a routine of training with the army and flying shipping reconnaissance sorties. Meanwhile the situation in Palestine deteriorated and, in July, Zionist terrorists blew up the King David Hotel in Jerusalem, killing more than 90 people.

In August the squadron received three Griffon-engined Spitfire FR.XVIIIs; replacement of the Mk.IXs had begun. They were fitted with three F20 cameras, one with a 14in (35.5cm) lens mounted as a port oblique and two with a 20in lens mounted vertically.

By the end of 1946 most of the wartime pilots had left and the majority of the new intake were inexperienced 'first tourists' with an average age of 21 – so fighter reconnaissance experience was very limited.

Early in 1947 the British Government made it clear that Palestine was essential to the security of Egypt – which, at the time, was Britain's main military base in ➡

Below
The CO of 208 Squadron, Sqn Ldr C F Ambrose.

32 SQUADRON IN PALESTINE

Converting from Hurricanes to Spitfire Vs in April 1943, 32 Squadron moved to Tunisia in August, by which time it had graduated to Mk.IXs. By December it was in Italy, and also operating Spitfire VIIIs. By the following November it was exclusively a Mk.IX unit, then based in Greece.

The squadron made the transition to Palestine, initially stationed at Ramat David, in February 1945 and began to re-equip with Spitfire F.XVIIIs and FR.XVIIIs in April 1947. Moving to Nicosia, Cyprus, on March 24, 1948, it also detached Spitfires to Ein Shemer and Ramat David to help cover the British withdrawal from Palestine. While in Cyprus, 32 converted to de Havilland Vampire F.3s from July 1948.

The badge for 32 Squadron is a stringed hunting horn with the Latin motto Adeste Comites, which translates as 'Rally round, comrades'. Today, 32 is based at Northolt and flies Agusta A109 helicopters and BAe 146 jets on personnel transport duties.

Above
A Spitfire IX of 208 Squadron photographed from the rear turret of a Handley Page Halifax during the unit's last months in Italy, 1945.
KEY COLLECTION

the Middle East. Accordingly, strong force levels were maintained, including RAF squadrons. But it was clear that the internal security situation in Palestine was reaching a crisis point, so most of the RAF families were evacuated. On May 15, Sqn Ldr C F Ambrose DFC, a former Battle of Britain pilot, arrived to take command of 208 during this difficult period.

As the conflict continued there were few air defence or ground attack duties for the squadron but it was kept busy carrying out close liaison work with the army and police units in the field – where the regular appearance of Spitfires overhead acted as a powerful

deterrent to hostile action

In addition, 208 patrolled not only the oil pipelines but also the water pipeline from the coast to Jerusalem, a vital facility since there was only one well in Jerusalem. Meanwhile, sorties along the coast looking for illegal shipping movements remained a daily task.

In September, the United Nations put forward the 'Partition Plan', a solution that appealed to neither side. The Arabs, realising they would have to fight for their independence, intensified activities to 'acquire' vehicles, weapons and ammunition, exacerbating the already tense security situation.

EAST AFRICAN TOUR
There was some relief from the difficult situation in Palestine when 208 Squadron left for a tour of East Africa on September 1, 1947, the first visit there by RAF Spitfires. Organised to coincide with the anniversary of the Battle of Britain, it was fitting that Sqn Ldr Ambrose, one of the 'Few', led the unit.

The main purpose of the deployment was to exercise mobility and reinforcement plans, and two Douglas Dakotas and two Avro Ansons carried ground crew and support equipment.

The detachment of six Spitfires

offered the prospect of challenging cross-country flying over a variety of terrain. The route via Fayid (Egypt) to Wadi Halfa, Khartoum, Juba (all Sudan) and Kisumu (Kenya) could not be flown on internal fuel alone, and the aircraft were fitted with 90-gallon (409 lit) overload tanks giving 3-plus hours of endurance.

Completing the 2,300 mile journey from Palestine in four days, the squadron arrived at Kisumu on September 5, leaving one Spitfire in Khartoum with a broken propeller. After three days for servicing, the six

fighters left for Entebbe, Uganda, where, during the afternoon, 208 gave a flying display before a crowd of almost 8,000.

The Africans were wildly enthusiastic, some having travelled for more than 100 miles, and the show was enlivened when Flt Lt E Hughes gave a solo aerobatic demonstration. After a final flypast, the aircraft left for Kisumu, flying over Kampala in formation en route.

On September 10 the small RAF station at Kisumu opened to the public and the local population inspected the aircraft. Later, the Spitfires took off to give a display with Fg Off M E Heath, in TZ237, the last to get airborne. At 500ft (152m) his engine failed, but Heath managed to crash-land just outside the airfield boundary near the crocodile-infested Lake Victoria, suffering only minor injuries and avoiding the jaws of the reptiles. Badly damaged, TZ237 was struck off charge.

The display continued as planned, finishing with a solo aerobatic routine by the squadron adjutant, Flt Lt K B Wood. The crowd were impressed, not least by the rescue operation to recover Heath and his Spitfire.

In Kenya, demonstrations were given at Nakuru, and more than 15,000 people saw the displays at RAF Eastleigh, near Nairobi, where resident squadrons also performed. Battle of Britain Day was commemorated in Nairobi when many of the local dignitaries and senior officers were present.

The local press reported: "The highlight of the programme was the demonstration of formation flying by 208 Squadron. In perfect weather conditions the squadron, led by Sqn Ldr C F Ambrose, flew, in turn, practically every possible formation at only a few hundred feet over the airfield. The speed and ease with which the aircraft moved through the air impressed the natives

beyond description, and when Flt Lt J E Wood gave a daring display of aerobatic flying low over their heads, it was not until the aircraft was some hundreds of yards away that their cheers of admiration were heard."

On the 19th the unit left for Mombasa, in Kenya, for another performance before heading for Dar-es-Salaam (Tanganyika) and flying a display at Tanga en route. Continuing its tour, 208 headed for Zanzibar, an island off Dar-es-Salaam, on the 26th, becoming the first RAF squadron to visit.

In his post-deployment report, the Air Officer Commanding East Africa, Air Commodore N A P Pritchett, commented: "The Spitfires of 208 Squadron arrived over the airfield on time at 11:30 hours and gave their demonstration of air drill and individual aerobatics, after which they landed and lined up. His Highness the Sultan of Zanzibar was taken round and introduced to all pilots. The ⊗

Below
Children in front of Spitfire FR.XVIII TZ242 at Asmara.

"RAF REGIMENT ARMOURED CARS RUSHED TO THE SCENE AND CAME UNDER HEAVY FIRE FROM THE TERRORISTS OUTSIDE THE PERIMETER. EXPLOSIVES PLACED IN RADIATORS OR COCKPITS DESTROYED SEVEN SPITFIRES OF 32 AND 208 SQUADRONS."

Supermarine Spitfire 80 — POST WAR SERVICE

208 SQUADRON IN PALESTINE

In December 1943, 32 Squadron got its first taste of the Spitfire, in the guise of Mk.Vs, at El Bassa in Palestine. As the unit made its way up the Italian 'boot', it began converting to Spitfire VIIIs from August 1944.

Leaving northern Italy in July 1945 the squadron returned to Palestine, settling initially on Ramat David. In August 1946 its first Spitfire FR.XVIIIs arrived. After moving into Nicosia, Cyprus, on May 26, 1948, the unit deployed to Fayid, Egypt, in November that year. It converted to Gloster Meteor FR.9s in the spring of 1951.

Long associated with the Middle East, 208 Squadron reflects this heritage with its badge, a sphinx. Its motto - 'Vigilant' - sums up its fighter role. Today, 208 is part of 4 Flying Training School at Valley, Anglesey, flying HS Hawk trainers.

continue to the last day. The main tasks for 32 and 208 Squadrons' Spitfires until then would be road convoy protection and security for the oil and water pipelines.

There would be a gradual withdrawal from bases in the south of Palestine, with those units remaining until the end – including 208 Squadron – moving into an enclave around Haifa in the north and, from there, the final withdrawal in mid-1948.

The area included the airfield at Ramat David, which had already been closed but would be reactivated for the two fighter squadrons.

The plan was to vacate Ein Shemer at the end of April 1948, but increased fighting between Arabs and Jews caused the squadron to move to Ramat David on April 4.

The unit flew constant patrols as a show of force and on May 12 provided a close escort as a road convoy evacuated the Air Headquarters in Jerusalem. On the departure of the High Commissioner and his staff two days later, 208 joined 32 Squadron in a flypast as the party embarked on HMS *Euryalus*. Apart from the enclave at Haifa, Palestine was finally free from the British Mandate.

Right
A damaged Spitfire after the attack at Petah Tiqva on the night of February 25/26, 1946.

Sultan was particularly impressed and most charming to all those to whom he spoke."

The tour ended with an air display at Dar-es-Salaam on the 27th. Once again there was wild enthusiasm.

EVACUATION PLANS
It was something of a culture shock to return to Palestine, where the security situation continued to deteriorate. Planning for the evacuation of the RAF began in earnest in October 1947 when operational flying would have to

'ROGUE' SPITFIRES

The date for the final evacuation to Cyprus was fixed as May 22, when 208 would fly a final reconnaissance of the southern sector before departing. But six days before, the State of Israel was proclaimed – and the situation slid into open warfare.

The early morning peace at Ramat David was shattered at 06:00 on May 22. A Spitfire appeared overhead and dropped a bomb among the two rows of eight RAF Spitfires on the hard-standing. Pilots rushed to their fighters as a second Spitfire appeared on a strafing run, damaging more aircraft and sending personnel running for cover. Two of 32 Squadron's aircraft (TP373 and TZ220) were destroyed and eight others suffered bullet and shrapnel damage.

Immediately, a trio of 208 Spitfires took off. Fg Off T McElhaw recalled: "Made a dash for my parachute, hopped into the first kite I came to, hoping it was still OK, but was beaten to the runway by Pete [Flt Lt P Speller] and 'Woodge' [Flt Lt M. Woodyer], in spite of taxying out nearly airborne!

"Of course, everyone thought it was the Jews getting a quick one in and we roared over airfields in Palestine, looking for aircraft that might have just landed – no joy, however, because he had 15

minutes' start. 'Woodge' and Pete went down over Tel Aviv to have a look at the airstrip there and were met with heavy accurate Bofors [anti-aircraft gun] fire. One hit 'Woodge' and made a small hole in the bottom of the cockpit."

As the three RAF pilots returned, Fg Offs G Cooper and R Bowie took off to mount a standing patrol. At 07:30, just as three Dakotas were landing, the 'rogue' Spitfires returned and the CO came on the radio, telling his two pilots to engage them.

Bowie immediately attacked one, recognising the markings of the Royal Egyptian Air Force (REAF), and shot it down as the second dropped a bomb, destroying one of the Dakotas. (Likely KN423 of 78 Squadron – ED.) The raider escaped at ground level but Cooper closed in and shot it down. Then a third Egyptian Spitfire appeared and RAF Regiment guns damaged it, forcing the pilot to crash-land and be taken prisoner.

Shortly after 09:00 there was a third attack. McElhaw and Fg Off L Hully had replaced Bowie and Cooper and were patrolling over Haifa when two Spitfires attacked Ramat David. The RAF pilots were recalled and McElhaw engaged one of the raiders at very low level as it attempted to escape. He fired three short bursts and the Egyptian Spitfire immediately flew into the ground. McElhaw later said it was

the first time he had ever done any air-to-air firing.

His day was not over. Turning, he saw another Spitfire, checked its markings – green, white, green – and he and Hully engaged it. McElhaw fired a long burst and it dived into the ground.

STANDING FIRM

Following the frantic morning, six more RAF Spitfires arrived from Cyprus as reinforcements. The Egyptians immediately made a public apology, claiming their aircraft had intended to attack the Israeli-held airfield at Megiddo but had misidentified Ramat David, losing five Spitfires during the ill-fated attack. The incident was to spoil the long-standing and otherwise good relations between the RAF and the REAF.

Rather than head for Cyprus on May 22 as planned, departure was delayed to the following day to avoid any impression that the RAF had been driven out of Ramat David. Teams worked frantically to patch up the Spitfires – nine leaving for Cyprus, immediately followed by the ground crews aboard Dakotas.

So ended an unhappy period of occupation as the British withdrew from Palestine and the Jewish state of Israel was proclaimed, heralding many more years of turmoil in the region. ➔

Below
Rain was a feature of 208 Squadron's Asmara detachment.

> "PILOTS HAD INSTRUCTIONS NOT TO CROSS THE BORDER OR ENGAGE GROUND TARGETS UNLESS THEY CAME UNDER ATTACK."

During the squadron's short stay in Cyprus, personnel said farewell to Sqn Ldr Ambrose after his very successful tour, which was recognised by the award of the AFC.

Confrontation between Egypt and Israel soon arose and, in November, 208 moved to Fayid in the Suez Canal Zone to reinforce the fighter assets of the RAF's 205 Group. Following Israeli ground incursions into the Sinai, the unit flew reconnaissance sorties in the first few days of January 1949 which confirmed Israeli actions in Egyptian territory.

FROM BOTH SIDES

Four 208 Squadron Spitfires flew a tactical recce January 7, 1949. Pilots had instructions not to cross the border or engage ground targets unless they came under attack.

Fg Off Cooper led the formation with Pilot II F Close as his No.2 and Fg Off McElhaw and Pilot II R Sayers providing top cover. The formation had not been told that Egyptian Spitfires

would be operating in the area. As Cooper's formation was coming to the end of its reconnaissance it came under fire from Israeli ground forces which had been attacked a few minutes earlier by REAF Spitfires.

While completing a photographic run, Cooper was hit by ground fire and looked across to see his No.2 in flames. Cooper saw Close parachute to the ground: he survived and was taken prisoner.

Cooper then looked up to see *three* Spitfires above, not two, and hurriedly transmitted a warning. But it was too late. The third aircraft was Israeli and flown by Canadian war 'ace' Sqn Ldr J H McElroy DFC, who shot down the two in front of him in one pass. Sayers was killed; McElhaw baled out and was taken prisoner.

Sayers may have seen the approaching Spitfire before McElroy opened fire, but as the Israelis had painted the spinners of their aircraft the same red colour as 208's, Sayers could well have assumed it was Cooper that had come up to join them.

Realising he was now on his own, Cooper saw another red-nosed Israeli Spitfire, clearly marked with Star of David roundels. He later discovered that Chalmers 'Slick' Goodlin, the Israelis' chief test pilot, was flying it; he had joined the RCAF and flown Spitfires during the war before

transferring to the US Navy.

To avoid being shot down, Cooper applied full throttle to climb and use the superior performance of his Mk.XVIII against the lesser-powered Israeli Mk.IX, but it was soon obvious that ground fire had damaged his engine. At 15,000ft he rolled over to convert height to speed but Goodlin's more manoeuvrable aircraft had the edge and a burst of fire shattered the instrument panel and hit the engine, leaving Cooper with no option but to bale out. He was picked up by a Bedouin on a camel and reached the Egyptian Army Headquarters at El Arish after a 3-hour ride.

All four of 208's Spitfires – TP340, TP387, TP456 and TZ228 – crashed well inside Egyptian territory. Close and McElhaw spent three weeks in Israeli captivity, while Ronald Sayers' remains were eventually recovered for burial.

DISASTROUS AND UNEXPECTED

This episode was as disastrous as it was unexpected. At 15:00 hours, 15 Hawker Tempest FB.6s from 324 Wing at Deversoir, Egypt, took off to give cover to six of 208 Squadron's Spitfires – led by the CO, Sqn Ldr Morgan – searching for the overdue aircraft.

Israeli Spitfires attacked the formation and one Tempest was shot down and its pilot killed (Plt Off D C Tattersfield flying NX207 of 213 Squadron – ED). Confusion ensued because of the Spitfires' similar red spinners; the camouflage schemes were also the same so it was difficult to identify friend from foe. After the engagement, the formation re-formed, but the search had proved fruitless.

The incident generated worldwide comment. A ceasefire was called almost immediately and by the end of January hostilities between Israel and Egypt ended after a series of Egyptian defeats on the battlefield.

During the coming months, 208 continued routine training in tactical and photographic reconnaissance but more emphasis was placed on air combat and gunnery exercises.

The unit continued to operate with the army and on May 24, 1950 it headed for Khartoum en route to Asmara, in Eritrea, on the Red Sea. The following day nine Spitfires flew into Asmara where the airfield, at 8,000ft, was subjected to torrential rainstorms lasting for about an hour each day.

The squadron's deployment was to support both the locally based Royal Berkshire Regiment and the police, which were in action against Shifta bandits raiding villages, stealing cattle and raping women.

Continuously manned Eritrean police posts were scattered throughout the country, some reinforced by patrols by the Royal Berkshires which scoured the countryside. As well as assisting the police and army patrols, the Spitfires also provided a deterrent.

Pilots of 208 flew in pairs, checking on the police post before climbing to ensure radio contact to inform HQ of their observations. They also monitored panels laid by patrols that pointed in the direction of bandits and gave estimated distances. Weighted canvas bags, with messages from the pilot or instructions from the joint HQ, were thrown out of the cockpit to the ground forces.

The Eritrean detachment was a welcome change from the desert of the Canal Zone, the squadron remaining for three months. On return to Fayid, a two-seat Gloster Meteor T.7 was waiting for them. This was the beginning of 208's conversion to jets, although it would be some time before the last of the Spitfires departed.

Long-awaited fighter-recce Meteor FR.9s started to arrive, the squadron then completing conversion to the new jets. Pilots continued to fly both types until the Spitfires were flown away to 107 Maintenance Unit at Kasfareet, Egypt.

The last arrived there on April 17, 1951, signalling the end of the Spitfire's days in the Middle East. ●

"AS THE ISRAELIS HAD PAINTED THE SPINNERS OF THEIR AIRCRAFT THE SAME RED COLOUR AS 208'S, SAYERS COULD WELL HAVE ASSUMED IT WAS COOPER THAT HAD COME UP TO JOIN THEM."

PACKARD
POWER

Rolls-Royce engineers transformed an RAF Mustang in 1942, replacing the Allison V-1710 to create an exceptional high-altitude, long-range fighter, epitomised by the P-51D. The American Packard Motor

SPITFIRE XVI FACTFILE

Engine:	Packard-built Rolls-Royce Merlin 266 of 1,580hp (1,179kW)
Statistics:	Dimensions: Clipped span 32ft 8in (9.96m) Length 31ft 4in (9.55m) Height 12ft 7³/₈in (3.84m) Weights: Empty 5,894lb (2,674kg) Loaded 8,289lb (2,526kg) Performance: Max speed 405mph (652km/h) Service ceiling 40,500ft (12,344m)
Armament:	Four 0.303in machine guns and two 20mm cannons; or eight 0.303in machine guns; or four 20mm cannons and two 0.303in machine guns. One 1,000lb (474kg) bomb under the centre section
First flown:	Late 1943, Mk.IX MH850 converted to Merlin 266
Number built:	1,053 at Castle Bromwich

Issued to the RAF in July 1945, Mk.XVI RW396 did not enter service until April 1946 when it joined the Central Gunnery School at Catfoss and later Leconfield. It was written off in a forced landing in January 1949. KEC

Company had been granted a licence to build the Merlin – USAAF designation V-1650 – the year before and ultimately 55,523 examples were built both for the UK and USA.

The Packard-built Merlin 266 (the equivalent of the British-made Merlin 66) was fitted to what was a slightly refined Mk.IX, available increasingly as a teardrop canopied 'low-back'. This was designated the Mk.XVI, the number change being deemed essential so engine spares and auxiliaries unique to the variant were not confused with their Mk.IX counterparts.

Norfolk-based 602 (City of Glasgow) Squadron was the first RAF unit to operate the Mk.XVI, from November 1944. Production, all at Castle Bromwich, finished in the summer of 1945. The Mk.XVI had a long career with the RAF, the last ones retiring from second-line duties in 1951.

Above
Issued to the RAF in the summer of 1945, Mk.XVI RW382 it was retired in 1953 and became a 'gate guardian' at Leconfield and later at Uxbridge. It was used as a 'static' in the 1969 film 'Battle of Britain'. Historic Flying restored it and it flew again in July 1991, moving to the USA four years later, only to suffer an accident in 1998. Returning to the UK, it was restored at Biggin Hill, flying in September 2013, wearing the colours of the Dutch 322 Squadron, which operated Mk.XVIs from late 1944 to October 1945. JOHN M DIBBS – PLANE PICTURE COMPANY

FIGHTER-BOMBER PUNCH

With the Mk.XIV filling the gap, the considerably refined Mk.XVIII was being developed. Fitted with a 2,035hp Griffon 65, the Mk.XVIII boasted a beefed-up airframe, greater fuel capacity, a bubble canopy as standard and fighter or fighter-recce

SPITFIRE XVIII FACTFILE

The camera port close to the roundel identifies SM843 as an FR.XVIII. The first production example, it saw no operational service, flying on test work from June 1945 to March 1953. KEY COLLECTION

Engine:	Rolls-Royce Griffon 65 or 67 – Griffon 65 rated at 2,035hp (1,518kW)
Statistics:	Dimensions: Span 36ft 10in (11.23m) Length 33ft 3¼in (10.14m) Weights: Empty 6,846lb (3,105kg) Loaded 8,862lb (4,020kg) Performance: Max speed 437mph (703km/h) Service ceiling 41,000ft (12,497m)
Armament:	Two 0.303in machine guns, two 20mm cannons. Up to three 500lb (227kg) bombs, on wing stations and under centre fuselage; or rocket projectiles
First flown:	July 6, 1945, first production example, SM843, flown at High Post by G P Shea-Simmonds
Number built:	300 by Supermarine
Sub-Variants:	F and FR versions

fittings. Park a Spitfire I alongside a Mk.XVIII and it is hard to believe they are blood relatives: only seven years separate their debuts.

World War Two had finished by the time Mk.XVIIIs were ready for issue to the RAF, but the variant went on to see its share of action. The first unit to receive the Mk.XVIII was 208 Squadron in Palestine in August 1946. As related in *Between A Rock And A Hard Place* on page 66, the unit had the surreal experience of combat with both Egyptian and Israeli Spitfires. In Malaya Mk.XVIIIs were used for strikes against communist terrorists during Operation FIREDOG. An attack on Kota Tinggi in Johore on New Year's Day 1951 by four Mk.XVIIIs of 60 Squadron was the occasion of the last time an RAF Spitfire expended weaponry in operational service.

Above
Based at Humberside Airport, Mk.XVIII SM845 (G-BUOS) is operated by Richard Lake's Spitfire Ltd. It was shipped to India in January 1946 and transferred to the Indian Air Force in December 1947. Like TP280, it was salvaged in the late 1970s, initially moving to the USA. Restored by Historic Flying at Audley End, it took to the air again in July 2000. JOHN M DIBBS - PLANE PICTURE COMPANY

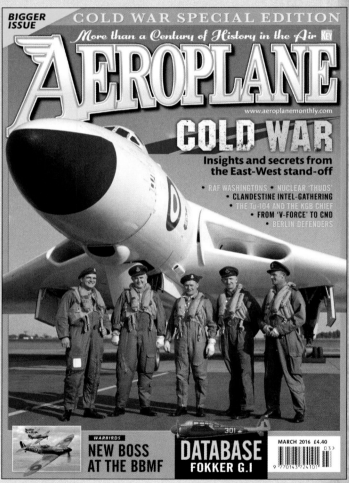

ALONE, UN
AND 'IN H

Flying long distances at high altitude to pinpoint targets is challenging at the best of times. To do this over enemy territory for most of the sortie in an unarmed, single-engined aircraft required a special breed of pilot. Such men faced demands of the highest order in World War Two, often succeeding where others might have given up.

In the early days there was no cockpit heating and pilots had to endure intense cold during flights that could last as long as six hours. Their only defence was to fly high, never stop scanning the sky and hope to outmanoeuvre any enemy fighter.

ARMED RM'S WAY

There was also another dimension to the men of the RAF Photographic Reconnaissance Units (PRUs). Unlike a fighter pilot or a bomber crew, whose job might be completed even if they failed to return, a photo-recce operation was useless if the pilot did not come back with a film that could be used by the image interpreters. Failure would mean another man would have to fly the same sortie the next day, when enemy defences would be more alert.

The work of the PRUs attracted little publicity and the pilots tended to be more mature than the popular conception of men in their late-teens or early 20s. Their job was more akin to that of a detective who returned repeatedly to a target to identify changes, and in this way an accurate intelligence picture could be drawn up. They would be the last to claim that they were 'special' but, to those who relied on their results, they were.

PEACEFUL WARRIOR

Gordon Hughes started his flying career with the London University Air Squadron before joining the RAF in July 1939 to complete his training. Initially he flew Avro Ansons and Blackburn Bothas on coastal patrols and anti-shipping sorties.

Born into a Quaker family, Hughes had an aversion to armaments and in February 1941 volunteered to join 1 PRU. The unit's Spitfire PR.ICs were not armed, allowing for extra fuel to increase their range. Soon after, the PR.ID arrived giving even greater range; later designated the PR.IV, it was to be the backbone of the PRU for the next two years.

Hughes became a great exponent of subtlety, instead of fire-power, to avoid being intercepted. He was once asked if he regretted not having armament in his Spitfire: "Oh no! That's the thing about PR. It's the only frontline job in this war where you aren't asked to kill. Your weapons are the cameras." ⏩

Below
A Spitfire PR.IV of 1 PRU.

"...PILOTS HAD TO ENDURE INTENSE COLD DURING FLIGHTS THAT COULD LAST AS LONG AS SIX HOURS. THEIR ONLY DEFENCE WAS TO FLY HIGH, NEVER STOP SCANNING THE SKY AND HOPE TO OUTMANOEUVRE ANY ENEMY FIGHTER."

Right
Gordon Hughes, who proved that cameras were a form of weapon.

Right centre
Hughes returning to San Severo after a sortie over Italy.

Below right
Freddie Ball at Maison Blanche. JIM BALL

"HUGHES ALSO TOOK A GREAT INTEREST IN THE ASSESSMENT OF HIS PHOTOGRAPHS AND ALWAYS VISITED THE INTERPRETERS TO DISCUSS RESULTS AND NEW TACTICS."

A perfectionist, Hughes planned his sorties in great detail and his CO described him as his finest pilot. His philosophy for survival was to make life as difficult as possible for the Luftwaffe. He flew as high as he could, remaining just below the level where condensation trails would form and enduring as much cold as possible, assuming most German pilots would not venture so high.

To that end, Hughes became a fitness fanatic so that he might have a bit more stamina than his opponent to endure long periods at high level. He also took a great interest in the assessment of his photographs and always visited the interpreters to discuss results and new tactics.

During a three-month period in the spring of 1941 he visited Brest and the Cherbourg Peninsula on 61 occasions to monitor the movements of the warships *Scharnhorst* and *Gneisenau,* frequently encountering heavy anti-aircraft fire. Later in the year he monitored targets on the Baltic coast and in Germany. Assessed as "exceptional and a most press-on type of pilot", he was awarded the DFC in August.

PR.XI: SECOND GENERATION SPY
In October 1941, the six flights of 1 PRU became 541, 542 and 543 Squadrons. But the personnel still considered themselves part of the PRU until the end of the war.

After a rest, Hughes became a flight commander on 540 Squadron, equipped with de Havilland Mosquitos. He flew many very long-range sorties over Europe, often searching for the German navy's capital ships sheltering in Norwegian fjords or Baltic ports, and was one of the first to photograph the German's secret experimental station at Peenemünde. He was awarded a Bar to his DFC and then a DSO.

On promotion to wing commander he returned to Spitfires in December 1943 to take command of the recently formed 336 Photographic Wing, part of the Mediterranean Allied Air Forces and based initially at La Marsa in Tunisia. Two of the wing's four squadrons equipped with Spitfire PR.XIs, sometimes described as the 'Second-Generation Spies'.

Operating over Italy, the Mk.XIs were sometimes used in the tactical reconnaissance role, when their long focal-length cameras were less effective – so a pair of additional F.8 cameras with 5in focal length lenses were fitted, one under each wing in a blister fairing. Hughes disliked this arrangement, believing high-level Spitfires were unsuited to tactical work and too valuable in their long-range primary role.

He had little time to savour North Africa. Soon after joining, the wing moved to San Severo in southern Italy, significantly extending its range into enemy territory.

The wing's Spitfires and Mosquitoes ranged over all southern Europe and on June 25, 1944 Hughes reached the furthest when he visited Ulm in southern Germany. He also photographed the huge Romanian oil installations at Ploesti.

Towards the end of 1944 he returned to Britain, but his Spitfire days were not over and he joined 34 (Reconnaissance) Wing, attached to the Second Tactical Air Force at Melsbroek, near Brussels. On March 25, 1945 he photographed targets in Denmark, his 192nd and final reconnaissance sortie.

Two days before the end of the war in Europe, Hughes was piloting an Anson which crashed, and he was badly injured, spending the next eight months in hospital. He left the RAF at the end of 1946 but joined the Royal Auxiliary Air Force and flew Spitfires and Meteors with 601 (County of London) Squadron. Gordon Hughes died in June 2012.

EXPERIENCE COUNTS
Many of the early PR pilots started their operational career in the army co-operation role, as was the case with Cranwell-trained Freddie Ball. He flew Westland Lysanders with

13 Squadron and escaped from the beaches at Dunkirk during the withdrawal of May and June 1940.

He volunteered for PR duties and, as they required experience on Spitfires, persuaded a friend to allow him to fly three sorties. At his interview Ball told the squadron commander he was an experienced Spitfire pilot and, to his surprise and joy, was accepted. He joined 1 PRU in May 1941.

Early sorties were to the Channel ports, but he was soon given targets deep in Germany. In October he flew into an embedded thunderstorm and at 25,000ft (7,620m) the aircraft became uncontrollable and he attempted to bale out, but the canopy jammed. The turbulence became so violent that he was thrown through the canopy. He recovered consciousness at 3,000ft and opened his parachute to land in Norfolk.

In November 1941 his unit was ordered to St Eval in Cornwall to fly daily sorties to Brest to monitor the *Scharnhorst, Gneisenau* and *Prinz Eugen*. The Luftwaffe became familiar with the tactics of the high-flying Spitfires and set up patrols to intercept them. Always prepared to challenge old practices and be innovative, Ball devised his own ploys, flying in from different directions, diving from very high level or transiting at low level and climbing at the last minute to take his photos.

Late in the afternoon of February 11, 1942 he found the trio of German capital ships still at Brest, surrounded by destroyers and minesweepers and apparently ready to sail. He photographed them, the last sighting before they sailed a few hours later on their audacious 'Channel Dash'.

From Cornwall he flew sorties to the Spanish border, covering the French Biscay ports. Assessed as an exceptional reconnaissance pilot, he was awarded the DFC.

CAPTURING BERLIN

At the end of his detachment to St Eval, Ball returned to his home base at Benson, Oxfordshire, from where he flew deep into Germany. On one occasion he had to fly eight overlapping runs over Berlin from 28,000ft. Two fighters appeared but he managed to lose them in patchy cirrus cloud before resuming his task and the long return flight home.

On promotion to squadron leader, Ball was made CO of a new unit, 4 PRU, and in October he left for Gibraltar to provide support for Operation TORCH – the invasion of French North Africa. Within days

3011 NA/243 682 P.R.Sqdn. MAY 29th.1943 1430 F/14 27,000'

Left
Venice as captured by Ball. VIA JIM BALL

Below
Hughes relaxing on the leading edge of this Spitfire at Benson.

his six Spitfires flew repeatedly over Algiers, Oran and Casablanca.

Losses to the enemy mounted and the 22-year-old Ball sought an audience with Air Chief Marshal Sir Arthur Tedder to plead for the latest Spitfires. Tedder listened patiently then dismissed Ball and told him to carry on his work. A few days later, three of the latest variants arrived.

On December 17, 1942, Ball was tasked to reconnoitre a crucial target in the Mateur area of Tunisia prior to a large-scale army attack. As he completed the task at 24,000ft, four Focke-Wulf Fw 190s closed in on him. He fought off eight attacks, despite his aircraft being hit, before finally escaping.

Forced to land at a forward airfield near Bone, Ball commandeered a Spitfire from the resident squadron and flew back to base with his film. Within hours, the ground forces staged a successful attack.

For his work in North Africa he was awarded the DSO and the US Air Medal. The DSO citation described him as a "fine leader who displayed brilliant airmanship".

FLYING-BOMB TARGETS
Ball returned from North Africa in July 1943. Six months later he was commanding 542 Squadron with Spitfires at Benson. His most urgent task was to monitor the construction of V-1 flying-bomb launch sites in the Pas de Calais. Prior to the Normandy invasion he photographed enemy dispositions and movements and, after the landings, identified targets ahead of the Allied armies' advance into Germany.

On his final Spitfire sortie the engine failed over Cologne at 38,000ft. He was able to coax short bursts of power during the long glide to England, breaking cloud at 600ft over the

Thames Estuary and scraping into Eastchurch.

On promotion to wing commander in September 1944, he took over 540 Squadron to fly Mosquitos to targets in Norway and into Germany.

He remained in the RAF and retired as an air marshal in 1979. Sir Freddie Ball died in January 2012.

DON'T PRANG ONE
Tim Fairhurst joined the Territorial Army in 1936 and was commissioned into the 7th West Yorkshire Regiment. With little activity after the outbreak of war, he responded to a request for army officers to transfer to the RAF to train as pilots – and completed his training in November 1940 when he was posted to 4 Squadron with Lysanders.

Frustrated by the lack of action, Fairhurst volunteered to join the PRU, which suited his temperament and sense of adventure. The only recollection he had of his first interview with his CO, Wg Cdr Tuttle, was being asked if he had flown a Spitfire. When he answered 'no', Tuttle responded: "Well, if you prang one, you're out." (At that point Fairhurst had never flown an aircraft with a retractable undercarriage, let alone a Spitfire!)

Starting operations with the PRU in September 1941, Fairhurst flew many long-range sorties over Germany and Norway. On many occasions his oxygen supply froze and he was forced to squeeze the tube to his mask to release the ice, enabling him to breathe again. Once, he flew for six hours and landed with five gallons of fuel remaining.

In the aftermath of the decimation of Convoy PQ 17 in Arctic waters off Norway in the summer of 1942, Fairhurst was summoned to see his station commander. He was told that he was to lead a top-secret operation

to locate the German fleet. There was also a requirement to photograph the ports in the area, but with the PR aircraft available it was impossible to do so with sorties mounted from Scotland.

ARCTIC BASE
Arrangements had been made to fly to the Russian airfield at Vaenga on the Kola Peninsula. Three Spitfires fitted with vertical and oblique cameras, and extra fuel tanks, were assigned to the operation supported by a small ground party.

Fairhurst prepared a plan for the 1,200-mile (1,931km) flight. He was first amused, and then dismayed, to find the maps for the region supplied by the RAF contained large blank areas marked 'uncharted territory'. He commented: "The White Sea was plain enough, so we would head straight for it when the town of Kandalaksha would provide a pinpoint, and then we would turn left to find the airfield at Afrikanda before flying on the next day to Vaenga."

Three Spitfires set off at

541 Squadron with Spitfires. By the end of the war he had flown 88 long-range PR sorties. Twice mentioned in despatches, Fairhurst was awarded the Belgian Croix de Guerre avec Palme.

After two years as a civilian, he re-joined the RAF in May 1947 and flew Spitfires in Malaya before going to Hong Kong. Tim Fairhurst finally retired from the RAF in 1965 as a wing commander, and died in April 2009. ●

"...CLOUD COVERED NORTH RUSSIA AND FAIRHURST WAS RELIEVED TO SEE THE WHITE SEA WHEN HE LET DOWN BELOW THE OVERCAST. THE TRIO LANDED AFTER A FIVE-HOUR FLIGHT."

five-minute intervals on September 1 with Fairhurst leading Fg Off D R M Furniss and Plt Off G W 'Sleepy' Walker. The weather was clear over Norway but cloud covered North Russia, and Fairhurst was relieved to see the White Sea when he let down below the overcast. The trio landed after a five-hour flight.

After arrival the Spitfires' RAF roundels were replaced with red stars. On September 10, Fairhurst took off on the first 'op' and headed for the fjords of northern Norway with the prime object of locating the *Tirpitz*. He photographed the capital ships *Admiral Scheer* and *Admiral Hipper* and the cruiser *Köln*, but the main objective had moved further south.

Following a bombing attack on their airfield on September 9, one of the Spitfires was damaged and a few days later Sgt D R Hardman arrived with a replacement. Over the next few weeks, Fairhurst and his pilots continued to keep track of the ships as the convoy PQ 18 headed for Murmansk.

On September 27, Walker was forced to low level due to low cloud over his target and two Messerschmitt Bf 109s shot him down over Banak. He is buried at Trondheim.

During a lunch with General Kutznetzov, the commander of the region, German bombers again attacked Vaenga. Fairhurst stood on a balcony next to the general, who grabbed a radio and personally directed Russian fighters as they tried to intercept the enemy.

As the raid departed, the lunch was continued. The general later inspected the Spitfires, which were to be left behind for the Russians, and expressed his dismay that such good fighter aircraft did not carry guns.

Fairhurst and his small party returned to Britain by sea on October 23 and shortly afterwards he was awarded the DFC.

After his Russian adventure, he went to the USA to brief the USAAF on PR operations before returning to the reconnaissance world, first on Mosquitos and then in command of

LONG-LASTING
PHOTO-R

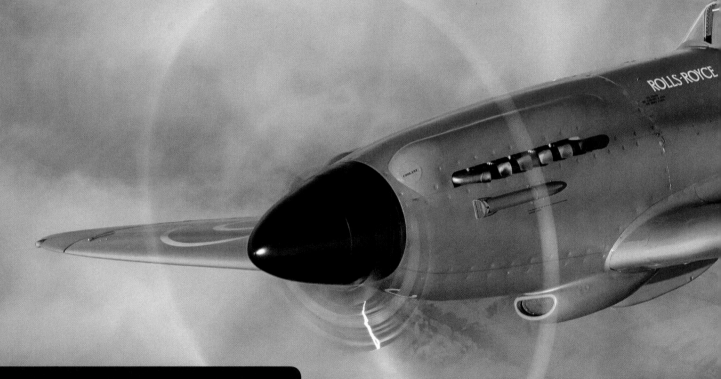

Always intended as an interim photo-reconnaissance (PR) platform, the PR.XI took the brunt of RAF single-engined sorties during World War Two. The ultimate PR Spitfire was the Griffon-engined Mk.XIX, which was based on the Mk.XIV. It began development flying in October 1944. An initial batch of 20 unpressurised examples was followed by a production run of 205 fully pressurised versions.

This is a good place to remind readers the many variants of the Spitfire encouraged a major change in the designation system in 1944. Roman numerals (eg Mk.XVI) continued but once Mk.XX had been reached, the change was made to Arabic, hence Spitfire Mk.21 etc. In

SPITFIRE XIX FACTFILE

Engine:	Rolls-Royce Griffon 65 or 66 of 2,035hp (1,518kW)
Statistics:	Dimensions: Span 36ft 10in (11.23m) Length 32ft 8in (9.96m) Height 12ft 8in (3.86m) Weights: Empty 6,522lb (2,958kg) Loaded 9,000lb (4,082kg) Performance: Max speed 445mph (716km/h) Service ceiling 42,600ft (12,984m)
Armament:	None
First flown:	Unpressurised RM626 tested from April 1944. Full prototype SW777 flown by G P Shea-Simmonds from High Post, October 1944
Number built:	225 by Supermarine

Above
Based at East Midlands Airport, near its headquarters in Derby, Rolls-Royce has operated PR.XIX PS853 since 1996. Widely renowned as an ambassador for Rolls-Royce, PS853 appears at airshows and also charity and corporate events. Not only does it represent the heritage of the Spitfire and the Rolls-Royce engines that powered them, it honours the pilots of all nations who flew them and the men and women who built and maintained them. It is civil registered as G-RRGN, the 'RR' being self-evident; 'GN' being the drawing number prefix for Griffon components. Delivered to the Central Photographic Reconnaissance Unit at Benson in January 1945 the following month it joined 16 Squadron in Belgium, later moving to Celle, Germany. Today, PS853 is painted in the colours of 'C' of 16 Squadron. In July 1950 it joined the 'Thum' Flight and was destined to become a part of the nascent Battle of Britain Memorial Flight.
BOTH JOHN M DIBBS – PLANE PICTURE COMPANY

ECCE

1948 the decision was taken to adopt Arabic numerals no matter what. For example, Spitfire PR.XIXs became PR.19s.

Interim unpressurised PR.XIXs first entered RAF service with 542 Squadron at Benson in June 1944. It fell to 81 Squadron at Seletar, Singapore, to carry out the last operational flight by an RAF Spitfire, on April 1, 1954; PS888 with the name The Last painted on the cowling, doing the honours. All was not over for the 'Nineteen', the type soldiering on with the civilian-operated 'Thum' Flight until 1957 – see *Founding Fathers* overleaf.

PS853

FOUNDING FATHERS

Above
Spitfire PR.XIX PS853 during its brief time with the Central Fighter Establishment at West Raynham, 1958. KEC

Right
Battle of Britain Flight Hurricane II LF363 and a pair of Spitfire PR.XIXs (PS853 nearest the camera) leading a trio of Lightning F.1s in a sortie out of Coltishall, 1963-1964. Top and bottom are Lightnings of the Wattisham-based 56 Squadron while in the middle is XM165 of Coltishall's 226 Operational Conversion Unit. KEC

It was as though they didn't want to go. Their work complete, three Spitfire PR.XIXs were due to depart RAF Woodvale, near Southport, to begin a new life with what was to become the present-day Battle of Britain Memorial Flight. The trio were due to leave on June 12, 1957 bound for Duxford but PS915 refused to start, PM631 took off, suffered a radio failure and returned, and PS853 took off only to come back with engine trouble; during its landing role it ended up ignominiously on its nose.

These were the last 'working' Spitfires in the RAF. They belonged to the Temperature and Humidity Flight operated under contract by Short Brothers and Harland. Spitfire PR.XIX PS853 had carried out the last weather-reconnaissance sortie on June 10, bringing an end to an era that had begun with the delivery of Mk.I K9789 to 19 Squadron at Duxford on August 4, 1938.

The celebrations were put on hold at Duxford and on June 14 two days late PM631 and PS915 successfully 'escaped' from Woodvale. Work on PS853 was completed on June 26 and, after an air test, it finally departed to the southeast.

DAILY CLIMB

Reliable weather information has always been a basic need of aviators. In April 1951 a fleet of five specially modified Spitfire PR.XIXs began to gather at RAF Hooton Park on the southern banks of the River Mersey, ready for service with a new, contractor-operated unit.

On May 1 the Temperature and Humidity Flight was officially formed and performed its first information-gathering sortie. 'Temperature and Humidity' was what the Spitfires were 'hunting' but it was an unwieldy title so it was contracted to 'Thum'. ➡

Above
Spitfire PR.XIX PM631 of the Battle of Britain Memorial Flight visiting Shawbury in August 1977. It is wearing the colours of 11 Squadron. KEC

Left
Thum Flight PR.XIX PM631, probably at Liverpool Airport. PETER GREEN COLLECTION

Below
Spitfire PR.XIX on its nose at Woodvale, June 12, 1957. KEC

LAST OF THE 'WORKING' SPITFIRES: THUM FLIGHT PR.XIXs

Serial	Fate/Current Status
PM549	While returning to Woodvale with radio trouble on May 4, 1952, it stalled on approach. Fg Off Ken Hargreaves was killed.
PM631	Airworthy with Battle of Britain Memorial Flight, Coningsby. In 541 Squadron colours
PM652	Encountered engine problems and crashed while attempting a forced landing near Shrewsbury, March 4, 1954. Flt Lt Tommy Hayes DFC was killed.
PS853	Airworthy with Rolls-Royce, East Midlands Airport, Derby. Civil registered as G-RRGN.
PS915	Airworthy with Battle of Britain Memorial Flight, Coningsby. In 81 Squadron colours, named *The Last!*

Below
During 1964 the Binbrook-based Air Fighting Development Squadron of the Central Fighter Establishment conducted air combat trials between Lightning F.3 XP696 and Spitfire PR.XIX PS853 of the Battle of Britain Flight. At the time there was a real threat of conflict with Indonesia and tactics needed to be developed in case Lightnings should confront that country's P-51 Mustangs.
PETER GREEN COLLECTION

The stay at Hooton Park was brief and on July 13, 1957 the Spitfires made the short flight up the Mersey to settle at Woodvale. One of the PR.XIXs carried out the daily weather sortie, landing at the new base.

The PR.XIX had been chosen because of its considerable endurance, stable flying characteristics, pressurised cockpit and the space, previously occupied by cameras to house weather instruments. Within the space behind the cockpit a balanced bridge psychrometer and an aneroid barometer were installed. The former used 'dry' and 'wet' bulbs to measure humidity and the latter recorded atmospheric pressure.

The flight profile, usually involving a daily departure at 09:00 hours, was a climb to 30,000ft (9,144m). Readings were taken at regular intervals and the pilot would make notes of weather conditions encountered. At the top of the climb, the Spitfire would make a descent to land at Liverpool Airport, Speke, where the data was off-loaded and whisked to the Central Forecasting Office at Dunstable for distribution to the RAF and civil authorities.

These sorties required exacting flying and lots of concentration. The daily gleaning of weather data was not without risk; two pilots were killed while flying Thum Flight Spitfires, see the panel opposite.

Keeping the Spitfires serviceable became increasingly difficult and so it was that PS853 flew the historic last sortie on June 10, 1957. At Woodvale Mosquito TT.35s and Meteor F.8s took over the task, the Thum Flight being absorbed into 5 Civilian Anti-Aircraft Co-operation Unit, also resident at Woodvale, in January 1958. Ultimately instrumented balloons took over from aircraft.

NEW ROLE

Duxford was only an interim stop for the former Thum Flight Spitfires. Amid great pomp Gp Capt J E 'Johnnie' Johnson, Gp Capt James Rankin and Wg Cdr Peter Thompson flew them in a close 'vic' formation to Biggin Hill on July 11, 1957. There they joined Hurricane II LF363 as the Historic Aircraft Flight, tasked with flying the aircraft at special occasions, including the annual flypast over London to mark Battle of Britain Day.

Spitfires were destined to have a long post-war service with the RAF, but the Hurricane's retirement was much faster, having been mostly withdrawn from service by 1947. At Thorney Island near Portsmouth, Hurricane II LF363 had been placed on charge with the Station Flight in 1948 so it could be used for the annual London 'run' on September 15; by 1956 it was based at Biggin Hill.

The prospect of three airworthy Spitfires becoming available was not overlooked and as Thum Flight wound down, the surviving trio were readied for a new role as a flying memorial to 'The Few'.

Initially known as the Historic Aircraft Flight, the Hurricane and PR.XIXs became the 'founding fathers' of the Battle of Britain Flight on February 21, 1958. After a somewhat gypsy-like existence, the flight settled on Coltishall in 1963 and there took on its present title the Battle of Britain Memorial Flight (BBMF)— in March 1976.

All three of the PR.XIXs are still airworthy — PM631 having given uninterrupted service since 1957. A review of the BBMF fleet led to the disposal of PS853 and in 1996 it became a civilian — registered G-RRGN — with Rolls-Royce and is regularly flown at airshows, special events and corporate occasions.

After delivery to Biggin Hill in July 1957, PS915 was retired the following month for 'gate guardian' duties at West Malling, Leuchars and Brawdy. During 1984 the PR.XIX was taken to British Aerospace at Samlesbury, near Preston, where it was restored to flying condition. Taking to the skies again in November 1986, PS915 caught up with BBMF and its colleagues PM631 and PS853, at Coningsby, where the flight has been resident since 1976.

Having had the honour of being the last 'working' Spitfires in RAF service, nearly 60 years on, PM631, PS853 and PS915 still enjoy acting as a tribute to the heritage of the RAF, Rolls-Royce and Supermarine. Not bad for a trio that exhibited considerable reluctance to leave Woodvale! ●

"THE PROSPECT OF THREE AIRWORTHY SPITFIRES BECOMING AVAILABLE WAS NOT OVERLOOKED AND AS THUM FLIGHT WOUND DOWN, THE SURVIVING TRIO WERE READIED FOR A NEW ROLE AS A FLYING MEMORIAL TO 'THE FEW'."

FlyPast

Your favourite magazine is now available digitally.
DOWNLOAD THE APP NOW FOR FREE.

FREE APP
with sample issue
IN APP ISSUES £3.99

SUBSCRIBE & SAVE

Monthly £2.99
6 issues £19.99
12 issues £34.99

SEARCH: FlyPast

Read on your iPhone & iPad Android PC & Mac kindle fire Blackberry Windows 8

SEARCH
BRITAIN AT WAR

FREE APP
with sample issue
IN APP ISSUES £3.99

SEARCH
AEROPLANE

FREE APP
with sample issue
IN APP ISSUES £3.99

ALSO AVAILABLE FOR DOWNLOAD

NEW Aviation Specials App FREE DOWNLOAD

How it Works.

IN APP ISSUES
£3.99

Simply download the FlyPast app and receive your sample issue completely free. Once you have the app, you will be able to download new or back issues (from September 2010 onwards) for less than newsstand price or, alternatively, subscribe to save even more!

Simply download to purchase digital versions of your favourite aviation specials in one handy place! Once you have the app, you will be able to download new, out of print or archive specials for less than the cover price!

Don't forget to register for your Pocketmags account. This will protect your purchase in the event of a damaged or lost device.
It will also allow you to view your purchases on multiple platforms.

 Available on iTunes Available on the App Store Available on Google play Available on BlackBerry Available on kindle fire  Available on PC, Mac & Windows 8

Available on PC, Mac, Blackberry, Windows 8 and kindle fire from **pocketmags**.com

Requirements for app: registered iTunes account on Apple iPhone 3G, 3GS, 4S, 5, 6, 6s, iPod Touch or iPad 1, 2 or 3, iPad Air, iPad Mini. Internet connection required for initial download. Published by Key Publishing Ltd. The entire contents of these titles are © copyright 2016. All rights reserved. App prices subject to change. Prices correct at time of going to press. 161/16

At first, the Supermarine design office tackled the problem of folding the Spitfire's wings by a complex arrangement that had the wings swivel from the trailing edge to lie pointing aft alongside the fuselage – in a similar manner to the Fairey Firefly. This was abandoned and the 'double fold' was perfected for the Mk.III – illustrated. Seafire II MA970 was converted and first flew in November 1942. With the Mk.III, the Seafire truly became a sea-going fighter; over 1,000 were produced.
ALL KEY COLLECTION UNLESS NOTED

HOOKED
AND FOLDED

A PORTFOLIO OF SEAFIRES – THE NAVAL VERSION OF THE SPITFIRE

The second prototype Seafire XV, NS490, carrying out dummy deck landings at the Supermarine test airfield at High Post. The Mk.XV was the first Griffon-engined Seafire and it started trials early in 1944. This example was initially built with a V-frame arrester hook underneath the lower fuselage, but by November 1944 it was busy testing a 'sting'-type hook mounted behind the tailwheel and below the truncated rudder. After trials on the grass at High Post, it was flown on and off the deck of HMS 'Pretoria Castle'.

Above
The view from the 'island' of HMS 'Indefatigable' as it sails into Wellington Harbour in December 1945 with the crew ranged to port and Seafire IIIs of 887 Squadron lined up. KEC

Below
Developed from the Mk.XV, The Seafire XVII was readily identified by its teardrop canopy and cut-down rear fuselage. Appearing in mid-1944, the Mk.XVII was destined for a long life with the Fleet Air Arm, ending its days in the mid-1950s with the reserve squadrons. Issued to service in December 1945, SX273 served with 741 Squadron at St Merryn as 'S-50' 1946-1947.

Above
In the final days of World War Two, Sqn Ldr G J Murphy flying with 887 Squadron from HMS 'Indefatigable' shot down a pair of Mitsubishi A6M 'Zeros' 30 miles south of Tokyo on August 15, 1945. During this exploit, Murphy was flying Seafire III NN212 '112-S'. On January 22, 1946, with another pilot at the helm, NN212 floated over the arrester wires on the deck of 'Illustrious' and engaged the 'barrier' – a net stretched across the deck to catch over-runs. The pilot was unhurt but the Seafire was never repaired. KEC

Left
Built at Castle Bromwich, Spitfire V BL676 was paid for by the Dutch West Indies Spitfire Fund and named 'Bondowoso', after a village in Java, during a ceremony in December 1941. It was sent to Air Service Training at Hamble and converted into a Seafire II, with arrester hook and a tropical filter and was sent for trials at Boscombe Down (illustrated) in April 942. By 1944 it was with 787 Squadron, the Naval Air Fighting Development Unit, wearing 'Royal Navy' titles and the serial MB328.

First flown on December 5, 1945 from South Marston, Seafire F.46 LA542 served at the Supermarine test airfield at High Post to evaluate the carriage of drop tanks and rocket projectiles, among other duties. It was issued to 778 Squadron in 1946. Developed from the still-born F.45, the Mk.46 and the more refined Mk.47s marked the final evolution of the Seafire.

Members of the press were invited to Yeovilton in August 1950 when Royal Navy Volunteer Reserve units from Bramcote (1833 Squadron) and Stretton (1831) flew down in readiness for deck landing training on the carrier HMS 'Illustrious' in the English Channel. Prior to deploying to the vessel, the photographers were treated to the spectacle of a deck landing officer (called a 'batman' for obvious reasons) conducting aerodrome dummy deck landings (ADDLs pronounced 'Addles') with the reservists' Seafire F.17s.

Below
Engine running on the rear of the flight deck of HMS 'Ocean', the aircraft of the 14th Carrier Air Group ready for an operation in the Mediterranean in late 1948. Centre and left are two Seafire FR.47s of 804 Squadron; the remainder being Fairey Fireflies of 812 Squadron. The Firefly unit operated mixed variants, the NF.1 all-weather fighter (with deep radiator 'chins') and fighter-recce configured FR.4s.

Right
While carrying out deck landing practice on HMS 'Ocean' during a Mediterranean cruise on October 29, 1948, the pilot of Seafire FR.47 VP435 skipped the arrester wires and was stopped by the 'barrier' – a net designed to catch errant over-runs. This resulted in a nose-over, but no serious injuries. The Seafire, from 804 Squadron and shore-based at Eglinton, Northern Ireland, was just ten months old, having flown for the first time at South Marston the previous January. It was not repaired and struck off charge in November 1948.

BEWARE OF PROPELLERS

TAKING THE LEGEND TO SEA

Hooked and Folded on page 92 deals with the evolution of the Spitfire from a land-based interceptor into the Seafire – a sea-going, wing-folding, hooked fighter capable of operating from carriers in the worst of weathers and sea states. Adapting the beautiful

Above
Britain's latest 'Spitfire' to take to the air is an incredible rebuild of the pioneering Seafire III. Westland-built Mk.III PP972 (G-BUAR) completed a long-term restoration and first flew on June 15, 2015. Issued initially to 809 Squadron in July 1945, it was transferred to the French Aéronavale in 1948 and flew combat sorties from the carrier 'Arromanches'. Cruising the Gulf of Tonkin, the carrier's aircraft assisted French Army units as they attempted to resist communist insurgent attempts to oust the former colonial power from Vietnam. Returned to France, PP972 morphed from instructional airframe, to scrapyard denizen to museum piece. It was brought to the UK in 1988 and moved around several locations in an 'on-off, on-off' restoration cycle. Moved to workshop in Suffolk, the miracle was finally completed and, painting in Fleet Air Arm South East Asian Command colours, PP972 turns heads wherever it goes.

Bottom right
Naval aviation specialists Kennet Aviation, based at North Weald, acquired Seafire XVII SX336 (G-KASX) restoration project in 2001 and was rewarded with a successful test flight on May 3, 2006. In doing so, the restoration team returned a Seafire to British skies for the first time in many decades. Accepted by the Fleet Air Arm in May 1946, SX336 saw no operational service and became an instructional airframe by 1953. Discovered in a scrapyard in Warrington in 1973, the Seafire began its long recovery to flight status. Today, it wears the colours of 766 Squadron. BOTH JOHN M DIBBS – PLANE PICTURE COMPANY

SEAFIRE III FACTFILE

Engine:	Rolls-Royce Merlin 55M of 1,585hp (1,182kW)
Statistics:	Dimensions: Span 36ft 10in (11.23m) Folded 13ft 4in (4.06m) Length 29ft 11in (9.12m)
	Weights: Empty 5,541lb (2,513kg) Loaded 7,197lb (3,265kg) Performance: Max speed 352mph (566km/h) Service ceiling 33,800ft (10,302m)
Armament:	Two 20mm cannon plus four machine guns. One 500lb (227kg) bomb under the centre section or two 250lb (113kg) bombs under the wings
First flown:	November 9, 1942, Seafire IIc MA970 converted as prototype
Number built:	1,180 by Cunliffe-Owen and Westland

With the 'A-frame' arrester hook tucked away under the rear fuselage the Seafire III could be taken for a classic Spitfire V. Westland-built Seafire III was evaluated by the Aeroplane & Armament Experimental Establishment at Boscombe Down during March 1944. The following month it was off to sea with 899 Squadron on the carrier HMS 'Ravager' on cruise to Gibraltar. KEY COLLECTION

and complex elliptical wing so that it could fold, enabling the Seafire to use little deck space and the lifts to take it below for maintenance, was an incredible feat of design and engineering.

With the Seafire III, the Spitfire truly went to sea, with the wing fold achieved just outboard of the wheel wells and the wing tips canting outwards to keep the overall height as low as possible. All Mk.IIIs were capable of being fitted with rocket-assisted take-off gear and later batches were configured for fighter-reconnaissance A Mk.II was converted to act as the prototype

in November 1942 and the first deliveries were made to 899 Squadron in the spring of 1944 and production was completed in early 1945.

The first Seafire variant with a Griffon engine was the Mk.XV, but this was always regarded as an interim type. The Mk.XVII was a considerable refinement of its predecessor with increased fuel tankage, a cutaway rear fuselage to greatly improve the efficiency of the arrester hook and a 'bubble' canopy. The version was built in either pure fighter and fighter-recce versions. The type became operational in September 1945 with 883 Squadron;

the last one rolled off the production line in October 1946.

Despite production and conversions amounting to just over 2,600 units, the number of surviving Seafires is small. Add the daunting challenges of working arrester hooks and the complications of folding wings have conspired to make airworthy Seafires very rare. The UK can boast two superb restorations, illustrating how the Seafire's development mirrored that of its 'land-lubber' brother with increasing aerodynamic sophistication and the change from Merlin to Griffon.

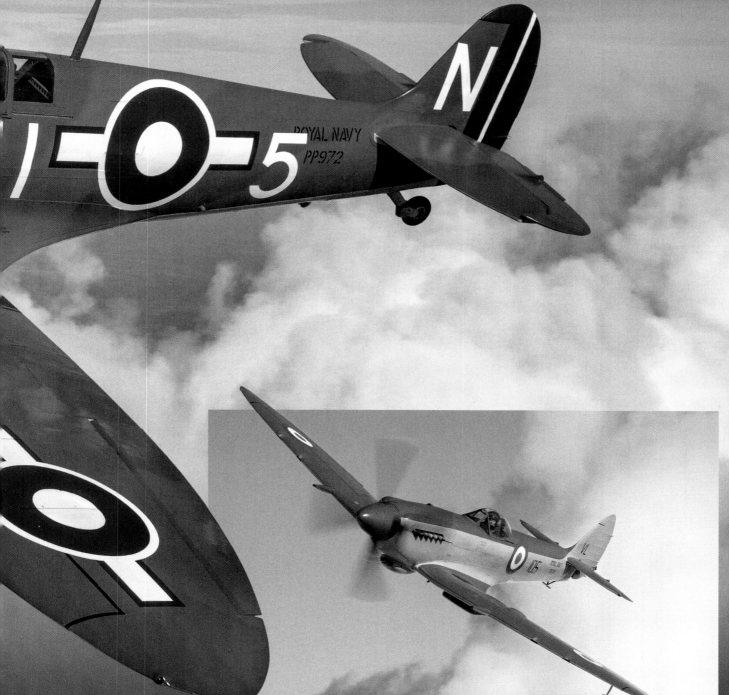

Supermarine Spitfire *80*

"THE SPITFIRE WAS VERY MUCH A PILOT'S AEROPLANE. IT HAD AN INDEFINABLE QUALITY OF EXCITEMENT ABOUT IT, AN UNMISTAKABLE CHARISMA, WHICH GREATLY APPEALED TO YOUNG AND EAGER PILOTS. IT WAS ALSO THE FASTEST AND HIGHEST-PERFORMANCE FIGHTER OF ITS DAY. IT IS TO THE ETERNAL CREDIT OF A GENERATION THAT TO BE A SPITFIRE PILOT BECAME THE DREAM AND PRIDE OF SO MANY OF ITS YOUNG MEN."

Jeffrey Quill in his superb *Spitfire - A Test pilot's Sortie*, rightly still in print and available from Crécy Publishing **www.crecy.co.uk**

Image: COL POPE